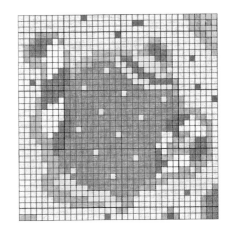

needlepoint

The **COUNTRY LIVING** Needlework Collection

needlepoint

projects · techniques · motifs

Karen Elder

Photography by Christine Hanscomb

Quadrille

page 1: Tea cosy (see page 36)
page 2: Patchwork stool top (see page 66)
page 3: Kelim cushion (see page 32)
page 5: Bobble-edged cushion (see page 40)

Illustrations • Kate Simunek, Tim Pearce,
Colin Salmon
Detail photography • Dave King

First published in 1996 by
Quadrille Publishing Limited
9 Irving Street, London WC2H 7AT

Published in association with the National Magazine Company Limited
Country Living is a trademark of the National Magazine Company Limited

Copyright © Text, design and layout 1996 Quadrille Publishing Limited
Copyright © Project photography 1996 Christine Hanscomb
Copyright © Detail photography 1996 Dave King

The right of Karen Elder to be identified as the author of this work has been asserted by her in
accordance with the Copyright, Designs and Patents Act 1988.

Art Director • Mary Evans
Art Editor • Vanessa Courtier
Project Editor • Hilary More
Copy Editor • Sarah Widdicombe
Editorial Assistant • Katherine Seely

British Library Cataloguing-in-Publication Data
A catalogue record for this book is available
from the British Library.

ISBN 1 899988 90 4

Printed in Spain

contents

Introduction

To embroider on canvas – or work a piece of needlepoint – is a simple craft. Projects can be elaborate, requiring skill and imagination to execute, or can be straightforward, for the most commonly used stitches are effective and easy to learn, and there is no particular need to explore further. The variety of patterns, yarns and canvases alone are enough to keep you occupied for a lifetime.

The hours fly by when you are engrossed in a piece of needlepoint. Over the centuries it has been worked as a pastime, but has not always been so exclusively the province of leisured ladies. The Bradford Table Carpet (early seventeenth century and now housed in the V&A Museum, London) was stitched in a workshop and is thought to have been not a commission but a product to sell. The amazing set of eighteenth-century chairs at Temple Newsam House in Yorkshire, is upholstered in needlepoint, and the skill of its stitching and vibrant colouring suggest that it was made professionally.

In the seventeenth and eighteenth centuries grand houses kept professional embroiderers who also drew up patterns for the ladies of the house to execute, for until the early 1800s commercial patterns were not available to buy. Their arrival from Berlin marked the beginning of a long rise in the popularity of needlepoint – or Berlin Work as it was called – in both England and the United States. The patterns were printed on squared paper and hand coloured, and the development of new dyes at around the same time created a fashion for brightly coloured floral patterns which is synonymous with Victorian taste.

Today we are spoilt for choice. Books have replaced the loose patterns of the last century and the detailed instructions and lavish illustrations they provide are both informative and inspiring. A wide variety of designs is also available packed into kits containing the wools, canvas and needles required. The difficulties of balancing colours for the designs has already been addressed, but with a charted (as opposed to printed) design the stitcher is still free to add colours or make adjustments to fit a particular need, which is one of the joys of this versatile craft.

Before you start

Choosing the materials for a needlepoint project is simple compared to embarking on a piece of surface embroidery. The appropriate canvas, thread, needle and whether or not you wish to use a frame, are all you need to consider when starting a project.

The stitches in a needlepoint project usually cover the canvas completely, so the selection of the base fabric is limited to quality and gauge. Most needlepoint is worked in wool or stranded cottons, and although there are several types available, the choice is not huge. It is wise to use proprietary yarns unless you are experienced, because they are made to withstand the harshness of running through the canvas and the twisting that sometimes occurs when stitching. They are also dyed to a high standard and available in an enticing array of colours, each brand offering a slightly different range of shades and thickness of thread. All are explained in this book.

materials & equipment

Needlepoint may demand little equipment, but it is important that the needle used is the right size and that the chosen thread covers the selected canvas. A comprehensive stock of small pieces of different gauge canvases on which to experiment with threads and stitches is an invaluable aid to successful and explorative stitching. A selection of frames (see page 12), although not always essential, can be extremely useful when working a piece of needlepoint.

The workbasket

The essential tools for needlepoint are a selection of needles, scissors, and a tape measure. A pair of small, sharp, pointed scissors is an absolute necessity for cutting threads close to the work. For cutting canvas, you will need a pair of large scissors. Some people like to stitch with a thimble. Apart from these basics, you will need:

• A waterproof marker, for marking the centre of the canvas and any outlines or measurements that may be needed. Use a pale-coloured marker when working with light yarn shades, to prevent the marks from showing through and spoiling the finished design.
• Masking tape, for binding the cut edges of the canvas to prevent it from fraying and snagging.

Canvas

Needlepoint canvas is a loosely woven, stiffened fabric usually made from cotton, although linen and synthetic fibres are sometimes used.

Gauge

Hugely varying effects can be achieved by using different 'gauges' of canvas: big, chunky cross stitch on large-holed canvas creates a fabric far removed in texture from the smoothness of tent stitch worked on a fine gauge.

The gauge is the number of holes per 2.5cm (1in) which may also be expressed per 10cm; the standard gauge range runs from 5 to 26 holes. All the canvases for the projects in the book are listed with their gauge. Changing the gauge will alter the size of the finished piece and change its character so work your projects on a canvas close to the original.

Widely available canvases:

Mono de luxe	White or antique	10–18 holes per 1in (40–70 holes per 10cm)
Interlock	White	10–18 holes per 1in (40–70 holes per 10cm)
Large interlock	Cream	7–8 holes per 1in (29–30 holes per 10cm)
Double thread (Penelope)	Antique	10 holes per 1in (39 holes per 10cm)
Double thread (thinner than Penelope)	White	10–14 holes per 1in (39–56 holes per 10cm)
Large double thread (Sudan)	Cream	4–5 holes per 1in (18 holes per 10cm)

Types of canvas

There are two main types of canvas: single thread and double thread.

Single-thread canvas

There are two kinds of single-thread canvas available:

• Mono, woven with single threads in the warp and weft.

• Interlock, woven with the weft twisted around the warp.

Both types are suitable for most needlepoint projects. However, half cross stitch (see page 23) is best worked on double-thread canvas, as it holds the stitches more centrally in the holes to give better coverage.

Mono de luxe canvas is the best quality, which is reflected in the price. The threads are polished to provide extra smoothness and it has the highest tension resistance, making it an ideal choice for chair seats and anything that will receive a lot of wear. It is available in both white and 'antique' brown.

Interlock is a strong canvas that is often used for kits, as it is easier to print a needlepoint design on than mono de luxe. Good-quality interlock canvas is suitable for most projects, but is mainly available in white.

Double-thread canvas

In double-thread canvas (sometimes called Penelope) the threads are laid two by two, and the working yarn is usually passed through the bigger holes. Details where tiny stitches may be called for can be worked by separating these double threads to make twice the number of holes, thereby doubling the gauge. However, be careful if your eyesight is poor as it is easy to push the needle through the wrong hole. Double-thread canvas is available in two shades, white and antique.

Plastic canvas

Plastic canvas is also available and is designed for making items which need sharp edges that cannot be turned under, such as tissue-box covers and spectacle cases. It is available in a variety of useful shapes, as well as by the metre (yard) and can be stitched right up to the edge which can then be oversewn to neaten with no further finishing required. Plastic canvas is available in several colours including transparent.

Choosing canvas

The canvas and yarn for a project must be selected to suit one another. The yarn should run through the holes in the canvas easily, but must also cover it completely. If the canvas shows through the work, then either the yarn is not the correct thickness for the gauge or the stitching is too tight.

Although canvas is described as an 'evenweave' fabric, with the same number of threads in each direction, you may find that there is a slight difference. Therefore, if you are planning to join two pieces of canvas you must make sure that the selvege runs in the same direction for both pieces.

As there are a number of canvas manufacturers, the quality can vary within the different types. Good canvas should not feel rough (over stiffened) and should not look hairy in the holes when held up to the light. Rough, hairy canvas will strip the yarn and does not feel good to hold. Although all canvas will fray with use, if it is already fraying in the shop it is best avoided.

Frames

A frame is an excellent aid to a good finish as it holds the canvas firmly during stitching. There are many types of frames available, and it is important that the one you choose is strong and does not bend or wobble.

Square or rectangular frames are the best for needlepoint.

It is important to decide how you will be sitting at your work – the choice is then narrowed down to a floor-standing frame or one that can be carried around. However, workstands are now available which will hold the frame so that you can have the best of both worlds.

Floor-standing frames

If you always work in the same place, you may consider using a floor-standing frame. Make sure you choose a sturdy, good quality frame which is the right height for the chair you sit in – your hands should not be so high that they cause your shoulders to rise.

Slate frames

Professional embroiderers use slate frames. These are not actually made of slate, but they are heavy and strong. The canvas is stitched on to webbing, which is then laced on to the side of the frame using strong thread, allowing the canvas to be pulled absolutely taut.

Stretcher frames

Stretcher frames are available from art supply shops (they are really intended for artists' canvases) and from some needlework shops. They are sold in pairs of sides which push together at the corners. You can buy a variety of lengths to create different frame sizes. The canvas is held on the frame with drawing pins.

Roller frames

Roller frames consist of two straight sides joined by two pieces of dowel, around which the canvas is rolled as it is worked. These frames are suitable if you are working in straight lines but not if you are using diagonal tent stitch, for the canvas will be tight where you have worked but loose where you want to stitch. As the work is rolled, you can only see a part of it at any one time.

Using a frame

When using a frame, find a position in which to sit where your back is not under strain and which allows you to use both hands for stitching. It is best to sit in an upright chair with both your feet on the floor. Unless you are using a floor-standing frame, sit at a table with the frame weighted down or clamped firmly to the edge.

Your left hand should be on the top of the canvas to push the needle down, with your right hand below to receive the needle and start the next stitch. This may feel strange at first, but once you get into the rhythm it begins to feel natural, and creates a beautiful tension.

Working without a frame

Many people stitch quite happily and successfully without a frame. However, for stitches that stretch over more than two or three threads of canvas it is advisable to use one, so that the canvas is kept flat and the right stitch tension created.

Canvas is stiffened in manufacture to help prevent distortion. If you crumple your canvas when working, the stiffening will break up and spoil it, so if you are not using a frame it is best to roll the canvas and hold the roll between the thumb and fingers of your non-stitching hand. This is comfortable and enables you to complete a whole tent stitch in one step – this is sometimes called 'scooping'.

Needles

Needlepoint is worked with tapestry needles which have a rounded point so as not to pierce the wool or canvas. They are designed to push gently through the fabric and past previous stitches, rather than through them. The needles are easy to thread as the eye does not need to be particularly fine to pass through the work. A packet of needles in assorted sizes is a useful standby in your workbasket.

Choosing the correct needle size will make your work comfortable to manage. Tapestry needles are graded from size 13, for use with the largest-holed rug canvas, up to 26, for use with the finest gauge. The most commonly used are:

Needle size	Canvas gauge
22	16
20	12–14
18	10
16	7–8

Yarns and threads

Wool and stranded cotton are the yarns most commonly used for working needlepoint. Silk is also suitable and wonderful to stitch with, but is expensive and not widely available. There are also numerous 'speciality' threads that are fun to use for detailing, or for adding highlights or a bit of sparkle. Beads will add another whole dimension, or can even be used in place of yarns to create 'beaded canvaswork'.

Needlepoint wool is usually packaged in skeins up to 10m (11yd) in length, or in hanks, which are larger and measured by weight. Check the label for length and weight, as these can vary. Stranded cotton is purchased in 8m (8¾yd) skeins.

Tapestry (needlepoint) wool

Tapestry wool comes as a single-thread. Single thread 4-ply tapestry wool is similar in weight to double knitting wool and is easier for inexperienced stitchers to use than stranded yarns. Most brands of tapestry wool are suited to canvas with 10–14 holes per 2.5cm (1in).

Crewel and Persian wools

Stranded threads (both wool and cotton) are extremely versatile, as you can adjust the number of threads to suit the gauge of the canvas. Crewel wool is a fine, single-thread yarn that can be doubled, tripled or more to suit different needs. Persian wool, so called as it was developed specifically for mending Persian carpets, is slightly thicker and more lustrous than crewel wool, and is made with three strands loosely packed together. The strands are separated easily to be used as required. You will need to experiment to discover what suits the canvas and the type of stitch you are using.

Stranded cotton

Stranded cotton is packed with six strands together. Beginners may find it difficult to get all the strands to run through the canvas evenly – using a frame will help.

Stranded cotton is widely available and can be used very successfully on canvas (see the Evening Purse on page 88). It looks like silk but is inexpensive by comparison, although it is more costly than wool. Stranded cotton is often used in conjunction with wool to work highlights, flower centres, French knots and so on.

Silk threads

Silk threads are not packaged to any standard length or thickness. It is therefore necessary to test silks for coverage and effect before embarking on a project using this beautiful yarn.

preparation

A little time spent in preparing your canvas and yarns can pay dividends in the long run. Canvas should be cut to the correct size, allowing a 5–7cm (2–3in) margin all round but no more, as it can become unwieldy. Binding the canvas edges with masking tape makes it comfortable to use, and it should be flat. Use an iron to remove any creases and to secure the tape. Finally, sort the yarns into colour groups and stitch a small piece of each colour into the margin to aid this process. In electric light, colours are easily mistaken and this reference can prove invaluable.

Using a chart

Needlepoint patterns for tent stitch can be translated successfully on to graph-paper charts, each square representing a stitch of the work. Note that a stitch goes over a canvas thread, from one hole to the next, not exactly as it looks on the chart – that is, the printed lines on the graph paper do not represent the threads of the canvas.

The designs in this book are presented on charts. In colour charts the colours may be exaggerated to provide visual differentiation and make them easier to follow. In black-and-white charts a symbol in each square represents the colour required. Some charts also include both symbols and colours.

Positioning the design

When embarking on an unprinted needlepoint project, the first step is to plan the placement of the design. Find the centre of the canvas by folding it in half horizontally and then vertically. The centre point is where the creases intersect. Identify the centre of the chart. Most charts mark the central axes with an arrowhead in the margin.

In order to follow a design without getting lost, it is a good idea to accentuate every tenth line on the graph paper, if it is not already darker. Mark the canvas in the same way, drawing a dotted line very lightly along the warp and weft of the canvas, using a pale-coloured waterproof marker. (**NB** Do not do this if you are using light yarn shades, as the marks may show through.) It is then easy to see where you are without continually having to count stitches.

Choosing a kit

When buying a needlepoint kit it is important to look further than the picture on the packet, for the quality of the materials inside can vary enormously.

A poor-quality or badly printed canvas is no fun to stitch. Straight lines in the pattern should be reasonably in line with the canvas, but as canvas is a loose-weave fabric there may be some 'wandering' of the line. This often worries people, but it should not be difficult to make the necessary adjustments as you stitch. Blurring of colours, or close shades printed in a way that makes them indistinguishable in electric light, is a much more serious problem. A good printer will give extra differentiation between the printed colours where wool shades are close; a good designer will also have thought through the printing process, rather than just producing a pretty pattern.

Getting the best from your kit

Firstly, sort out which wool shades relate to which printed shades. Most kits have little squares of colour printed on the canvas margin; knot a piece of the relevant colour into each square before you start stitching and then in artificial light you will not confuse the shades.

Always read the instructions. The designer may have used some surface stitching, or suggested alternative stitches for the background, which cannot be printed.

Transferring designs on to canvas

Printed and painted canvases are widely available, and charts are in good supply through magazines and books like this one. However, should you wish to trace or paint your own design on to the canvas, this is quite easy. To start with, it is best to use simple, freestyle images and shapes; more complicated patterns can be chosen when you have gained some experience.

Tracing

Tracing a design on to canvas gives outlines for guidance, but the positioning of colours is left to the stitcher to create freehand. Shading the design on paper to use it as a reference for colour placement is helpful.

You will need

Tracing paper
Black felt-tipped pen
Masking tape
Fine-tipped black or grey waterproof marking pen

1 When you have chosen your design, mark the centre and trace the design on to tracing paper with a black felt-tipped pen, concentrating on the important outlines. Fix the tracing on to a flat, clean, white surface using a few short pieces of masking tape.
2 Mark the centre of the canvas. Matching the centres fix the canvas down over the tracing, again using small pieces of masking tape.

3 Using a fine-tipped black or pale grey waterproof marker, lightly trace the design on to the canvas. You can now stitch this marked canvas, putting in the shading 'freehand'.

Painting

Painting a design on to canvas makes it straightforward to stitch. The paints or felt-tipped pens used for this must be waterproof. Tracing the design first can be helpful in ensuring that mistakes are not made.

You will need

Quick-drying, waterproof paint
Fine paintbrush, for details
Larger paintbrush, for more extensive areas of colour

1 If you are not confident of your artistic ability, paint or colour your design on to paper before painting the canvas.
2 Fix the design underneath the canvas in the same way as for tracing and paint it, following the colours on the paper.

from start to finish

Where to begin stitching and how to start and finish a thread are the most important, but often unexplained, fundamentals of achieving good needlepoint. Placing the first stitch into the canvas, happy in the knowledge that it is neatly done and will not come loose, is essential for the confidence of the stitcher. With a sure and relaxed hand the stitches will flow across the canvas with an even tension, resulting in a smooth and polished looking piece of needlepoint.

Threading needles

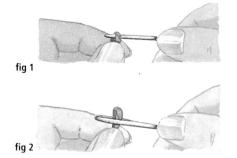

fig 1

fig 2

Threading a needle is something that many people find difficult because of poor eyesight or simply through not knowing an efficient way to do it. Needlepoint needles have large eyes and so are easier to thread than many fine embroidery needles. The easiest way to thread a needle successfully is as follows:

1 Hold the needle in your right hand (or left if you are left-handed) and, with your other hand, loop the thread over the point of the needle and pull it tight against the needle (fig 1).
2 Hold the loop firmly between your thumb and index finger, turn the needle around, place the eye over the loop and push it down so that the thread passes through it (fig 2). Do not lick the wool when threading the needle; it is an unpleasant experience and achieves little.

Where to start

fig 3

Where you start stitching a piece of needlepoint is important and can differ depending on the pattern and design of the needlepoint.

• For freestyle (as opposed to geometric) patterns, start with the main features. This probably means starting in the centre, and continuing outwards until all areas have been stitched.
• For geometric patterns, start at the top right-hand corner (fig 3) and work down the canvas towards the bottom left-hand corner, in a continuous flow.
• If there is a border to the design and you are not using a printed canvas, mark the border on to the canvas with a waterproof marker. Do not jump around when stitching, as you may find that the pattern does not join up successfully if a counting mistake has been made.
• When everything else has been worked to your satisfaction, stitch the background. Putting in the background last helps to smooth out any unevenness in stitching curves or thin lines. This can be the most exciting phase of the stitching, when everything takes on its proper shape and the colours are offset by the background shade. Start the background at the top (top right-hand corner if you are using diagonal tent stitch) and work downwards.

Starting a thread

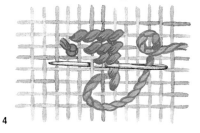

fig 4

The following method of starting is not only safe but beautifully neat and tidy too, as the thread is worked in underneath the canvas and is covered completely.

1 To start, thread the needle and make a knot right at the end of the yarn.
2 Push the needle down through the canvas about 2cm (¾in) away from where you wish to begin, leaving the knot on the front of the canvas.
3 Stitch towards the knot (fig 4), making sure that it is in the 'flight path' of your stitching (that is, the direction you will be going), and when you get near to it, snip it off. The thread underneath will have been neatly worked in underneath.

Threads should be started (and finished) within their own colour, so that bits of darker fluff do not get caught up with paler shades and spoil them.

Finishing a thread

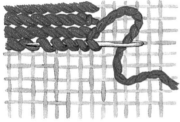

fig 5

The method used for finishing a thread firmly and neatly varies slightly according to whether you are using wool or stranded cotton.

• To finish a wool thread, simply run it under several stitches of the same colour at the back of the work (fig 5). Wool is quite sticky and stays in place when run under just a few stitches.
• Stranded cotton and silk need to be anchored more firmly. To finish a thread, run it under a few threads of the same colour at the back of the work, working first in one direction and then the other.
• Snip off all ends as you go to prevent colours from getting mixed up. The back of your work will then be neat and tidy.
• Never jump from one area of a colour to another, leaving long threads at the back – this will cause the tension to change and the colours will get mixed in with one another. It makes better sense to start and finish a new thread for each area worked.

Finishing threads on a frame
When using a frame, finishing a thread can be awkward, as turning the frame over may be difficult or impossible. A different method can be adopted:

1 When you have made your last stitch, bring the thread up to the front of the canvas a few stitches away from where you have finished, and at a point where it will soon be worked in.
2 Trim the thread to about 2cm (¾in), and when it has been worked in underneath, snip off, flush with the canvas top.

Achieving a good finish

Perfecting the stitch tension is the most important technique to master in order to achieve an even finish and a straight canvas. Tight tension can ruin a piece of needlepoint, while a soft, natural tension creates a beautiful and even finish and is relaxing to work. Resist the temptation to give each stitch an extra little tug as you pull the wool through – the wool is slightly elastic and the extra little tug will stretch it spoiling the stitch and pull the canvas badly out of shape.

The evenness of needlepoint stitches is made by two things: pulling the wool as you stitch, and the stitch that shares the hole of the one you have completed. Try to bring your needle up in an empty hole and push it down in a full one. When you push the needle down through a hole where there is already a stitch, the action gently smooths that stitch. If you start a stitch in a hole that already contains one, you may dislodge it. causing unevenness.

using this book

Chart keys
Colour keys are given with the charts for each project. In each key, the first column gives the colours and thread used for the original project and the second column gives the nearest equivalent colours in an alternative brand, although these can be very different.

Canvas gauges
In Britain and the United States, canvas gauges are still quoted using the number of holes per inch. See page 10 for a fuller explanation and the metric equivalents.

Thread quantities
Every stitcher uses a different amount of thread. The given quantities should be used as a guide only. Some of the pieces are old and the quantities only estimated.

blocking canvas

Canvas worked in tent stitch rarely stays truly in shape, and almost any stitching on canvas benefits from being stretched, or 'blocked', back into shape. Tightly stitched canvases that look messy and bumpy are improved enormously by some severe blocking treatment, while any slight unevenness in a well-stitched canvas should be quickly eliminated before transforming the stitched canvas into its final shape. Follow one of the methods shown here to achieve a smooth needlepoint piece.

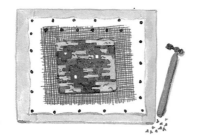

fig 1

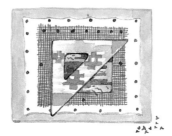

fig 2

You will need

Board at least 15cm (6in) larger in each direction than the finished piece
Piece of clean white sheeting
Sponge
Heavy-duty drawing pins, or carpet tacks for larger pieces
Hammer
Set square, or other item to give a right-angle

1 Pin the sheeting to the board to prevent any stain in the wood from discolouring the work.
2 Dampen the back of the needlepoint using a sponge, but do not saturate it.
3 Lay the needlepoint face down on the board. Pin or tack down the top edge in a straight line (fig 1). Position the pins or tacks in the unstitched canvas margin, about 2.5cm (1in) from the edge of the stitching. If the work is badly out of shape, you may need to put in a pin or tack every couple of centimetres (inch) or so. Put the first in the centre and work outwards in both directions.
4 Place pins or tacks in the centres of the other three margins, starting with the bottom one. Use the set square or other right-angled item to ensure that the corners are all at right-angles (fig 2). You may have to pull the canvas hard.
5 Once the work has been secured, leave for at least a week until thoroughly dry.

Blocking small pieces

There is an alternative, unconventional, but effective and less physically demanding method for pieces of work no larger than 50cm (20in) square, and if the needlepoint is dirty you may find that this process also helps to clean it.

fig 3

You will need

Wallpaper paste and brush
Artist's stretcher frame (see page 12) large enough to allow the canvas to be pinned on to it using the unstitched margin
Heavy-duty drawing pins, or carpet tacks for larger pieces
Electric kettle, or other equipment to produce serious steam
Rubber gloves

1 Mix a some wallpaper paste into a thick, non-watery solution and set aside.
2 Using two chairs, trestles or sturdy boxes, create a stand on which the frame can be placed flat over the electric kettle (with the lid off) or another steamer, so that the steam rises to heat and dampen the canvas from about 20cm (8in) below the canvas.
3 Pin the canvas on to the stretcher. The pins or tacks should be no more than 5cm (2in) away from the edge of the stitched canvas, closer if possible.
4 Place the stretcher over the kettle or steamer, with the stitching face down (fig 3). This should not be dangerous, but for safety's sake you should wear rubber gloves and ensure that your arms are covered, as the steam can scald. After about a minute in the steam the canvas should be pliable, and you will be able to pull the stretcher frame into shape until the canvas is perfectly square. Leave in the steam for another minute and then switch off the kettle or steamer.
5 Brush the wallpaper paste on to the back of the stitched area.
6 Leave flat for about a week to dry out.

caring & storing

Needlepoint should last for many lifetimes especially if good-quality materials and the correct stitches are picked for the chosen project. The biggest enemies are dust and sunlight. Although modern wools are colourfast to a high degree, over the life of a piece some fading must be expected. Leaving needlepoint in a sunny spot will certainly spoil the colours, so bear this in mind when placing pieces around the house, or displaying framed needlepoint pictures.

Cleaning

The best way to care for your needlepoint is to spray it well with a fabric protector as soon as it is made up and then use a vacuum cleaner on it regularly. Damping it or using solvents may remove the natural oils in the wool that are its best protection.

Only clean your needlepoint when it is really necessary – which is less often than you may think – and then send it to a good dry cleaner. Never wash your work: the canvas may shrink and the wool become matted, and if it is a printed or painted canvas there is a chance that the colour may run. In addition, washing removes the canvas dressing, which may be keeping the work in shape.

Storing

The best way to store needlepoint which will not be used for some time is to shake it well to remove any dust and then lie it flat (or rolled if it is a large or long piece) in a drawer, wrapped in acid-free tissue paper. Do not use plastic bags, as the static attracts dust and the textiles will not be able to breathe. Place a mothball in the drawer where it will not touch any of the fabric. Finally, lay a piece of cotton sheeting on top.

Tent stitch

The most frequently used stitch in needlepoint is 'tent' stitch, in which the canvas is covered by stitches that cross one thread of canvas diagonally. This is the most versatile of all the needlepoint stitches, and there is no need to learn more if you are happy with it, for there are whole worlds of shading, pattern, and colour manipulation to be explored using just this one stitch. Figurative, abstract and geometric patterns can all be formed successfully in tent stitch, and with experience its limitations become challenges of ingenuity and skill. Making straight lines appear to be curves, deceiving the eye with apparent textural effects and using imaginative shading techniques are just some of the fun.

working tent stitch

Tent stitch is formed by bringing the wool up through a hole in the canvas and down through the hole diagonally opposite. This stitch is also called *petit point*, but this is not, as the name suggests, a tiny stitch – nor is *gros point* a big stitch. *Petit point* is tent stitch and *gros point* is cross stitch, on canvas of any size.

People are sometimes timid about stitching details – especially curves in tent stitch – when using any but the finest gauge canvases. There is no need to use a 22 gauge to make a face or curve a petal, for it is an impression that is being created by needlepoint. A pattern stitched on a fine gauge will usually adapt to a large gauge, and vice versa.

There are three commonly used ways of forming tent stitch: diagonal tent stitch, continental tent stitch and half cross stitch.

Left handed stitchers

Most left handed people stitch using their right hand, working in the same way as right handers do. However, those who do stitch using their left hand may find it easier to work tent stitch with the stitches lying from top left to bottom right, rather than the more usual top right to bottom left. If using diagonal tent stitch, start at the top left hand corner of the pattern. If using continental or half cross stitch, start wherever it feels most comfortable. Finding the most comfortable way of stitching is probably the best advice. 'Right' and 'wrongs' are unimportant so long as the required effect is achieved and the sewer finds enjoyment when stitching needlepoint projects.

Diagonal tent stitch

Sometimes called 'basketweave' because of the pattern it creates on the back of the work, diagonal tent stitch consists of rows of stitching that run diagonally up and down the canvas on the 'cross' of the fabric, working towards the top of the design on the up row and towards the right-hand edge on the down row. Each stitch fills a gap between the stitches of the previous row.

1 Starting at the top right-hand corner of the area to be covered, bring the needle up through the canvas at the bottom of the stitch and down in the hole above and diagonally to the right (fig 1).
2 Make the next stitch parallel to the first and stitch the row going diagonally up or down the canvas as required. The small gaps between the stitches will be filled when the next row is worked.
3 Work the next row below the first (fig 2), bringing the the needle up in the empty canvas and down between the stitches of the row above (fig 3).

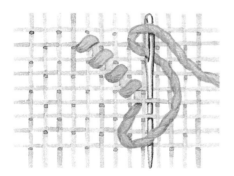

fig 1

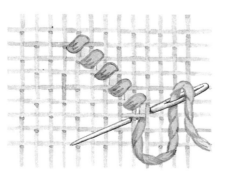

fig 2

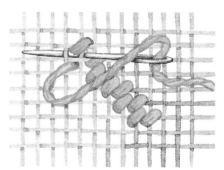

fig 3

Continental tent stitch

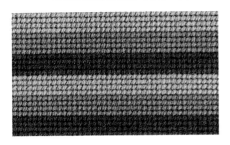

This variation consists of rows of stitching that travel in straight lines backwards and forwards across the canvas, creating a long diagonal stitch at the back.

1 Working the first row from right to left, bring the needle up through the canvas at the bottom of the stitch and down in the hole above and diagonally to the right (fig 4).
2 Making a long stitch at the back, bring the needle up again to the left of the first stitch, and continue.
3 Work the second row from left to right (fig 5), this time bringing the needle up through the canvas at the top of the stitch and down in the hole below and diagonally to the left (fig 6), making long, diagonal stitches at the back.

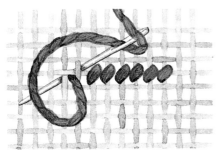

fig 4

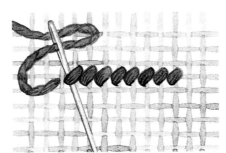

fig 5

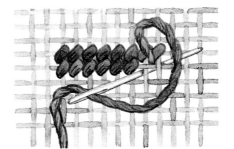

fig 6

Half cross stitch

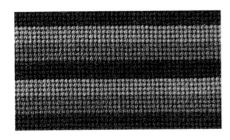

Technically, this method is not a tent stitch, but it looks the same on the front of the work. It is formed by stitching in straight lines across the canvas, but creating a short vertical stitch at the back.

1 Working the first row from left to right, bring the needle up through the canvas at the bottom of the stitch and down through the hole diagonally above and to the right (fig 7).
2 Making a small straight stitch at the back, repeat step 1.
3 Work the second row of half cross stitch from right to left (fig 8), bringing the needle up through the canvas at the top of the stitch and down in the hole below and diagonally to the left (fig 9) making small straight stitches at the back of the work.

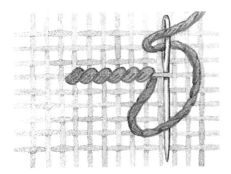

fig 7

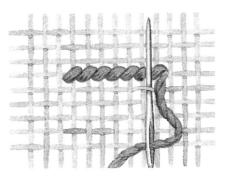

fig 8

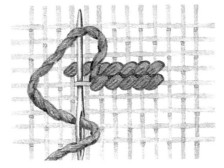

fig 9

boat pictures

Three little boat pictures, each framed using old pieces of wood with peeling paint, have an immediate, rustic appeal. They make a refreshing change from mass-produced frames and no two can ever be the same.

The designer is left-handed and he has therefore slanted the stitches from top left to bottom right, as opposed to the more usual top right to bottom left: either way works well. If you want to follow exactly what the designer has done, turn the work on its side so that the top left becomes top right.

Three fishing boats

About the picture

Approximate finished design size: 17cm x 7cm (6¾ x 3in). The picture has been stitched using Anchor tapestry wool.

You will need

14-gauge interlock or mono de luxe canvas, 27 x 18cm (10¾ x 7in)
Size 20 tapestry needle
Tapestry wool in the Anchor or Rowan colours as shown in the key below

To work all the needlepoint designs

The designs are all worked in tent stitch. The continental method is suggested, as the lined effect that it gives adds an appropriate texture to the seascapes. Stitch the boats first and then the backgrounds.

When stitching the steamer, use all six strands of cotton throughout. Frame the complete pictures.
NB The charts and keys for yacht and steamer designs are on pages 98 and 99.

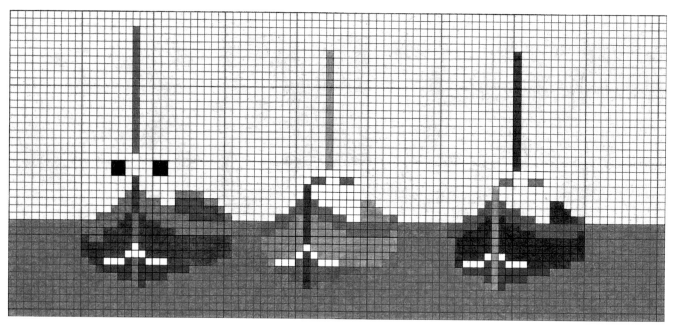

Tapestry wool	Anchor	Rowan	skeins
■ black	9800	A62	1
grey	9798	A625	1
soft grey	9764	Z61	1
■ dark greenish blue	8840	M54	1
■ cherry red	8220	G46	1

Tapestry wool	Anchor	Rowan	skeins
■ maroon	8512	H659	1
■ brown	9410	X146	1
■ soft brown	9392	J427	1
ginger	8062	D620	1
■ orange	8162	C618	1

Tapestry wool	Anchor	Rowan	skeins
☐ fawn	9362	A2	1
☐ white	8006	A110	1
☐ sky blue	8736	N422	1
■ sea blue	8738	N88	1
■ green	8880	P100	1

Yacht

About the picture

Approximate finished design of the blocked needlepoint picture: 7 x 9cm (3 x 3½ in).

The picture has been stitched using Anchor tapestry wool.

You will need

14-gauge interlock or mono de luxe canvas, 17 x 19cm (6¾ x 7½in)

Size 20 tapestry needle

Tapestry wool in the colours shown in the key (see pages 98 and 99)

Steamer

About the picture

Approximate finished design size: 8 x 4cm (3¼ x 1½ in).

The picture has been stitched using DMC stranded cottons except for the sea, which uses Anchor.

You will need

17-gauge interlock or mono de luxe canvas, 17 x 19cm (6¾ x 7½in)

Size 26 tapestry needle

Stranded cotton in the colours shown in the key (see pages 98 and 99)

25

circus cushion

The bold colours and inventive subject make this a lovely design for a playroom or child's bedroom. The three figures are made up as if from flip cards, depicting heads, torsos and legs that can be mixed and matched to create hundreds of different and unlikely characters. This humorous idea is set in a festive border of stars, circles, hearts and zigzags that defy boredom in the stitching. There is neither shading nor any complicated colouring, making this a good design for a beginner to tackle.

About the cushion

Approximate finished size: 34cm (14in) square. The cushion has been stitched using Anchor tapestry wool.

You will need

For the needlepoint:
10-gauge double-thread (Penelope) canvas, 50cm (20in) square
Size 18 or 20 tapestry needle
Tapestry wool in the Anchor or DMC colours shown in the key on page 28
For the cushion:
1m (1¼yd) medium-weight cotton furnishing fabric, 122cm (48in) wide
30cm (12in) zip
Sewing thread to match fabric
1.5m (60in) No 3 piping cord
40cm (16in) square cushion pad

To work the needlepoint

The design is worked in tent stitch, using any preferred method.

With this busy design there is no reason for any particular order of stitching, but the general rule is to work from the centre, so stitch the figures first and then their individual frames. Stitch

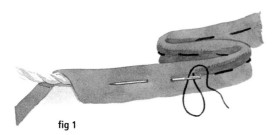

fig 1

the border when the whole central section is complete.

To make up the cushion

1 Block the completed canvas and trim the unstitched margin to approximately 2cm (¾in) all round.

2 Cut out 2 pieces of backing fabric 40 x 15cm (16 x 6in) and 40 x 30cm (16 x 12in).

3 Place the 2 pieces of fabric right sides together and lay the zip along the cut line in a central position. Mark where the zip starts and finishes, and machine stitch to the mark at each end, taking a 2cm (¾in) allowance.

4 Lay the fabric flat on an ironing board, face down. Press back the 2 short seams and the fold where the zip is to be inserted. Tack and then machine stitch the zip in place. Partially open the zip.

5 Cut one 6cm (2½in) wide strip of fabric on the cross (diagonally across the grain), approximately 7cm (3in) longer than the circumference of the cushion. With wrong sides together, fold the strip in half lengthways over the piping cord and tack to hold it in place (fig 1).

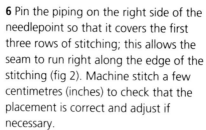

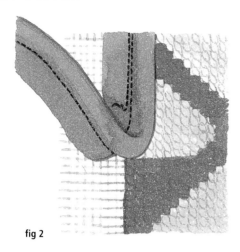

fig 2

6 Pin the piping on the right side of the needlepoint so that it covers the first three rows of stitching; this allows the seam to run right along the edge of the stitching (fig 2). Machine stitch a few centimetres (inches) to check that the placement is correct and adjust if necessary.

7 Machine stitch the piping in place all around the needlepoint, easing the piping around the corners and clipping the fabric so that it does not pull. Hand sew the ends together to fit.

8 With right sides together, pin and tack the backing fabric to the needlepoint. The piping will be caught in between and will cause the fabric to be quite tight across the back. Using a piping foot, machine stitch around the edge, keeping close to the piping.

9 Machine stitch again just around the corners, and then snip off the excess canvas and fabric quite closely.

10 Turn the cover right side out and ease out the corners, using a tapestry needle to pull them out gently if necessary. Insert the cushion pad and close the zip.

Tapestry wool	Anchor	DMC	skeins
cream	8004	Ecru	3
light yellow	8112	7471	3
bright yellow	8116	7433	1
red	8216	7666	3
bright orange	8166	7740	2
light orange	9444	7917	1
pale orange	9522	7171	3
pink	8394	7132	1
mauve	8524	7253	2
turquoise	8802	7828	2
peacock blue	8690	7317	1
charcoal	9768	7624	2
bright green	9154	7341	2

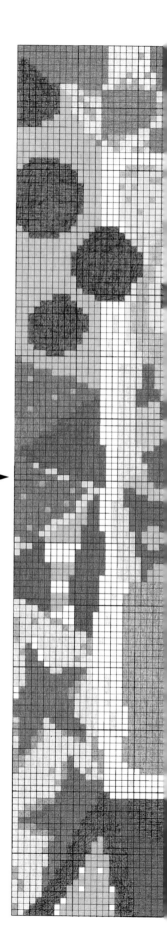

29

album cover

An album of memories is very personal, but most have rather boring or even ugly plastic covers that belie the contents. Giving an album an individual and hand-made cover makes it truly your own. This one is covered in a natural, coarse-weave linen fabric, with a strip of antique-looking needlepoint applied for decoration.

About the cover

Approximate finished motif size: 10.5 x 4cm (4¼ x 1½in)

The length of the stitched needlepoint strip should be the same as the height of the album. The instructions are for an album 28 x 30cm (11 x 12in). The album border has been stitched using Appletons tapestry wool. Adjust the quantities of the materials to suit the album of your choice.

You will need

For the needlepoint:

10-gauge double-thread (Penelope) canvas, 15 x 40cm (6 x 16in)

Size 18 or 20 tapestry needle

Tapestry wool in the Appletons or DMC colours shown in the key left

For the cover:

Photograph album

30 x 60cm (12 x 24in) lightweight polyester wadding

38 x 96.5cm (15 x 38in) natural linen fabric

1m (1¼yd) No 5 piping cord

7 x 75cm (3 x 30in) bias strip of red cotton fabric

Sewing thread to match fabrics

Fabric adhesive

Tailor's chalk

To work the needlepoint

The design is worked in tent stitch, and the diagonal method is recommended. Work the strawberries and leaves first, and then the background.

To make up the cover

1 Block the completed canvas and trim the unstitched margin to approximately 2cm (¾in) all round.

2 Make two 36cm (14¼in) lengths of piping following step 5 of the instructions for the Circus Cushion on page 26.

3 Pin and tack the piping along the edges of the canvas following step 6 of the instructions for the Circus Cushion on page 28. Machine stitch the piping in place.

4 Turn under and machine stitch a 1.5cm (½in) hem all around the linen fabric. With the right side out, wrap the fabric around the closed album, leaving 2 flaps of equal length protruding over the edges. Using tailor's chalk, mark on the fabric where the album ends.

5 Tack the needlepoint strip on to the fabric 5cm (2in) in from the marked edge. Machine stitch in position, placing the needle between the piping and the needlepoint edge. Alternatively, slipstitch by hand underneath the piping.

6 Fold back the 2 fabric flaps along the marked line (the needlepoint will be covered). Pin, tack and machine stitch each flap along top and bottom with a 2cm (¾in) seam allowance, to form 2 pockets. Turn these right side out and press to neaten seams and edges.

7 Glue the wadding to the album cover and allow to dry.

8 Slip the fabric cover over the album. Fold the fabric margin to the inside of the album spine and glue to hold the cover firmly in place.

Tapestry wool		Appletons	DMC	skeins
	dark green	548	7379	1
	olive green	347	7393	1
	mid green	345	7376	1
	light green	343	7362	1
	pale green	341	7424	1
	yellow	693	7472	1
	wine red	505	7199	1
	scarlet	504	7127	1
	red	503	7108	1
	light red	223	7851	1
	ecru	691	7491	3

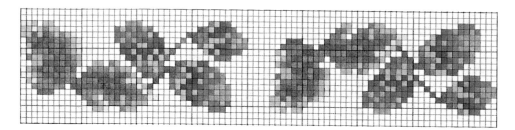

kelim cushion

Inspiration for creating successful needlepoint patterns is never far away, and traditional furnishings provide an endless source of suitable patterns. Indian rugs are especially rich in colours and geometric shapes that work particularly well in needlepoint, as they were designed for wool and therefore lose little in the translation from weaving to stitching.

About the cushion

Approximate finished size: 57 x 58cm (22¾ x 23in). The cushion has been worked using Appletons tapestry wool.

You will need

For the needlepoint:
7/8 gauge interlock canvas 70cm (28in) square
Size 16 tapestry needle
Tapestry wool in the Appletons or Anchor colours shown in the key on page 34
For the cushion:
60 x 65cm (24 x 26in) medium-weight furnishing fabric
Matching sewing thread
50cm (20in) matching zip
2.5m (3yd) cord furnishing trim (optional)
Buttonhole thread (optional)
65cm (26in) square cushion pad

To work the needlepoint

The design is worked in tent stitch. Use 2 threads of yarn in the needle to achieve the thickness required.
The pattern is built up in bands. Stitch one band at a time, working from the top right-hand corner across the canvas. Finish one band before starting the next, otherwise the pattern may not fit correctly. Rigorous counting of stitches is not necessary: the pattern is free and will not be upset by some 'inaccuracies'.

To make up the cushion

1 Block the completed canvas and trim the unstitched margin to 2cm (¾in).
2 Cut out 2 pieces of backing fabric 60 x 50 cm (24 x 20in) and 60 x 15cm (24 x 6in).
3 Insert the zip in the backing fabric following steps 3 and 4 of the instructions for the Circus Cushion on page 26.
4 With right sides together and the needlepoint uppermost, pin, tack and machine stitch the backing fabric to the needlepoint. The machine stitches should run down the middle of the last line of stitching. After sewing along one side, check that you have not encroached on the stitching and also that there is no unstitched canvas showing, and adjust as necessary.
5 Complete by following steps 9 and 10 of the instructions for the Circus Cushion on page 28.

To attach the trim (optional)

1 Snip the bottom seam of the cushion to make an opening 6cm (2½in) long.
2 Using buttonhole thread or sewing thread doubled, slip stitch the cord to the cushion, starting at the opening created in step 1 and stitching along the seam. The stitches should be made quite close together but should not be pulled tight, as this may cause the canvas to pucker. Leave 6cm (2½in) of cord free at each end for making a neat join.
3 When the stitching is complete, tuck the 2 ends through the opening.
4 Trim off the cord ends inside to 5cm (2in) and gently unwind the cord ends.
5 On the outside of the cushion, carefully overlap the cord ends where they meet to make a neat join, and hand stitch firmly in place.

Tapestry wool	Appletons	Anchor	skeins
biscuit	764	9492	9
custard	851	9522	12
deep yellow	474	8136	8
honeysuckle	696	8102	7
grey green	354	9174	2
deep green	294	9078	2
flamingo	626	8162	3
coral	866	8240	20
scarlet	505	8220	10
royal blue	821	8688	11
deep royal blue	823	8690	4
china blue	748	8634	18
marine blue	328	8840	11

35

tea cosy

This jolly tea cosy is a good project for a beginner as it is not too large and the motifs are simple, making it quick to complete. It is also a good piece for freeing the mind from the rigours of counted patterns, where every stitch must be placed correctly, and the freedom of the wavy border should discourage you from feeling that you have made mistakes if the stitching is not reproduced exactly as the chart indicates. The randomly placed dots in the background are a clever device for breaking up a plain colour.

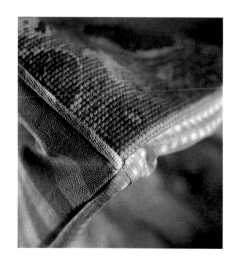

About the cosy

Approximate finished design size: 24 x 31cm (9½ x 12½ in). The tea cosy has been stitched using Anchor tapestry wool. Light blue gingham has been used to make up the tea cosy, and complements the design.

You will need

For the needlepoint:
10-gauge double-thread (Penelope) canvas, 40 x 45cm (16 x 18in)
Size 18 or 20 tapestry needle
Tapestry wool in the Anchor or DMC colours shown in the key on page 38
For the cosy:
50cm (20in) medium-weight cotton backing fabric, 90cm (36in) wide
Two 38 x 30cm (15 x 12in) pieces lightweight cotton, for lining
Sewing threads to match fabrics
70cm (28in) No 3 piping cord, (optional)
Two 38 x 30cm (15 x 12in) pieces medium-weight wadding

To work the needlepoint

The design is worked in tent stitch, and the diagonal method is recommended.

Stitch the motifs and the border first, then work the dark blue dots in the background. These require some long stitches to be carried over the back of the work, but the threads will be covered when the background is completed. You should avoid carrying over more than a couple of centimetres (inch) of loose thread. Finally, work the background.

To make up the cosy

1 Block the completed canvas thoroughly (it is very important that it is straight) and trim the unstitched margin to about 2cm (¾in) all round.

2 Make the piping from the backing fabric, following step 5 of the instructions for the Circus Cushion on page 26.

3 With the right side of the needlepoint uppermost, pin and tack the piping cord around the curve of the cosy. The tacking stitches should be positioned exactly where the machine stitching will eventually run. Make sure that no unstitched canvas is showing.

4 Cut a strip of backing fabric 14 x 6cm (5½ x 2½ in). Press raw long edges to the centre, then press in half. Topstitch 3 rows of evenly-spaced stitches along the strip. Fold in half to form a loop and pin to centre top of cosy over piping.

5 Place the needlepoint on the cotton backing fabric and mark around the edge using tailor's chalk, with a 2cm (¾in) seam allowance all round. Use this shaped piece of fabric to cut out 2 more pieces of lightweight fabric and wadding for the lining.

6 Place the needlepoint and backing fabric right sides together; the piping and loop will be sandwiched in between. Using a piping foot, machine stitch close to the edge of the piping. Remove any tacking stitches that may be showing.

7 Tack a wadding piece to one side of each lining piece. Stitch the 2 pieces of lining fabric together along the curve, leaving a small opening for turning. Then machine stitch bottom edges to bottom edges of the cosy. Turn the cosy right side out. Slipstitch the opening closed.

8 Push up the lining inside cosy. Hold with a few stitches at the top of the cosy.

Tapestry wool	Anchor	DMC	skeins
bright pink	8454	7603	1
red	8440	7849	1
orange	8306	7951	2
pale gold	8038	7503	2
bright yellow	8114	7431	1
green	9112	7382	1
pale green	9092	7400	1
turquoise	8802	7828	1
powder blue	8684	7800	5
sky blue	8644	7798	1
dusky blue	8628	7283	1
lilac	8586	7241	1
pale grey	9782	7300	1
cream	8032	Ecru	1

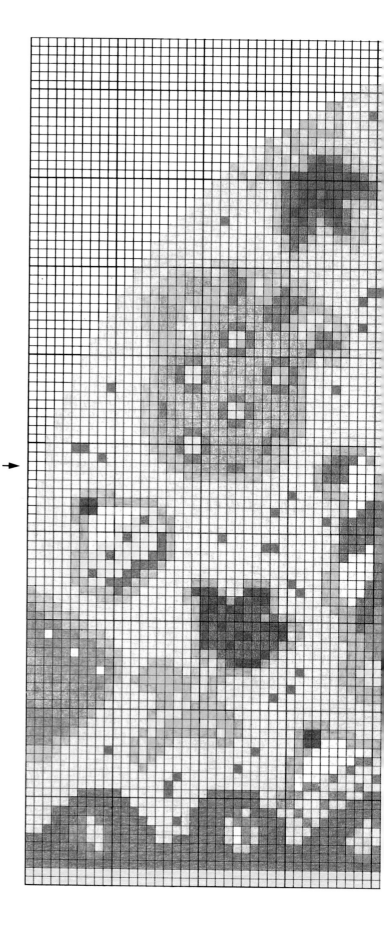

bobble-edged cushion

Oversized blooms, reminiscent of Dutch flower paintings, look wonderful in needlepoint and are especially suitable for upholstery, as the pattern can be used as a length of fabric rather than as a design. This bobble-edged cushion has been made up using this technique, and the pattern makes a welcome change from designs contained within borders.

The shading of the flowers and foliage is especially interesting. A very large number of colours has been used and the tones are often unexpected. For example, the big pink flower uses reds, greys, greens, yellow and white – with some pink. The overall impression, however, is not of a multi-coloured flower, but of a pink one with the underside of the petals darker than the top. The darker shades are also used for the leaves, and the red is employed again to shade the yellow flowers.

About the cushion

Approximate finished size 34cm (14in) square. The cushion has been stitched using Appletons tapestry wool. Rust red, ribbed Indian furnishing cotton has been used to make up the cushion.

You will need

For the needlepoint:
10-gauge double-thread (Penelope) 50cm (20in) square canvas
Size 18 or 20 tapestry needle
Tapestry wool in the Appletons or Anchor colours shown in the key on page 42
For the cushion:
50cm (20in) square of medium-weight furnishing fabric
30cm (12in) zip
Sewing thread to match fabric
1.5m (60in) bobble trim
40cm (16in) square cushion pad

To work the needlepoint

The design is worked in tent stitch, using any preferred method.

Work the largest flowers first, then the leaves and small flowers, and finally the background.

To make up the cushion

1 Block the completed canvas and trim the unstitched margin to 2cm (¾in).
2 Cut the backing fabric into 2 pieces and insert the zip, following steps 2–4 of the instructions for the Circus Cushion on page 26.
3 With right sides together and the canvas uppermost, tack and then machine stitch the backing fabric to the needlepoint. The machine stitches should run down the middle of the last line of stitching *unless* you are using a bobble trim (see below). After stitching along one side, check that you have not encroached on the stitching and also that there is no unstitched canvas showing through to the right side. Adjust if necessary.
4 Complete by following steps 9 and 10 of the instructions for the Circus Cushion on page 28.

To attach the trim

1 Make up the cushion as above, but instead of stitching down the middle of the last line of stitching, leave an unstitched canvas margin to match the width of the trim.
2 When the cushion is complete, stitch the trim over the unstitched canvas. To accommodate the corner, make a pleat or tuck in the trim. Fold under the cut ends before stitching down. Pin on the bobble trim before you start stitching and adjust to ensure that the bobbles are evenly placed at each corner.

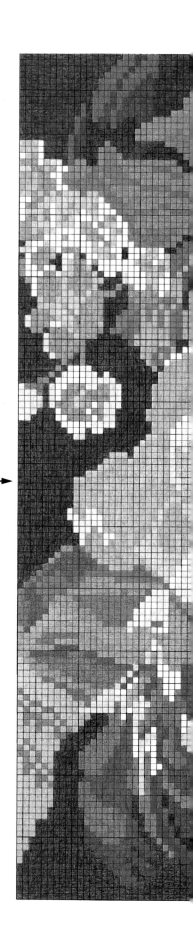

Tapestry wool	Appletons	Anchor	skeins
coral	866	8240	2
pale flame	204	8324	1
terracotta	124	9620	2
beige	121	9596	2
dark paprika	726	9564	1
paprika	725	9562	2
pale paprika	721	9512	1
bisquit	765	9448	2
fawn	912	9388	1
honeysuckle	695	8060	1
golden brown	903	9426	2
grey	962	9788	1
rose pink	141	9614	2
pale chocolate	181	9632	1
autumn yellow	476	9526	1

mid terracotta	223	8348	2
pale mauve	883	8582	1
ivory	871	8032	1
olive green	342	9054	1
dark green	358	9182	1
green	355	9176	2
grey green	351	9254	1
pale fawn	951	9364	1
jacobean green	298	9026	1
mid jacobean green	296	9082	1
beige green	292	9066	3
dark olive green	245	9220	2
blue	159	8906	3
deep yellow	475	8102	1

house, heart & hand cushions

Hands and hearts appear as motifs in the symbolism of many cultures. They are associated particularly with the American Shaker movement, one of their sayings being 'Hands to work and hearts to God'. The little schoolhouse motif is also associated with the Shakers and nineteenth-century American country-style folk art.

These designs must be worked with a stranded yarn, as the subtle, faded effect is created by splitting the strands and threading two different-coloured wools together in the needle.

About the cushions

Approximate finished size: 23cm (9in) square Each cushion has been worked using Paterna Persian yarn.

NB See pages 100 and 101 for the outline design for the heart and hand cushions. These can be worked using the same stranded wool colours as for the house cushion.

You will need for each cushion

For the needlepoint:
10-gauge double-thread (Penelope) canvas, 30cm (12in) square
Size 18 or 20 tapestry needle
Stranded wool in the Paterna or Appletons colours shown in the key for the house cushion on page 47
For the cushion:
Piece of denim approximately 3cm (1¼in) larger than the design all round
Matching sewing thread
Loose polyester wadding

Stranded wool	Paterna	Appletons	skeins
cranberry	940	948	1
spice	850	866	1
cranberry	940	948	1
dark rust	870	127	1
terracotta	482	721	1
spice	850	866	1
terracotta	482	721	1
pale rust	873	206	1
rusty rose	934	753	1
flesh pink	494	704	1
old gold	754	693	1
honey gold	735	692	1
honey gold	735	692	1
white	263	991	1
old blue	510	926	1
old blue	510	926	1
federal blue	503	322	1
glacier blue	563	741	3
blue	561	745	3

To work the needlepoint designs

The designs are worked in tent stitch - the diagonal method is recommended. Start with the central motifs and then stitch the backgrounds, combining wool colours together as shown in the key for a subtle faded effect. Use 2 strands of Paterna Persian yarn or 3–4 strands of Appletons crewel wool throughout.

To make up the cushions

1 Block the completed canvas and trim the unstitched margin to approximately 2cm (¾in) all round.

2 Right sides together with the stitched piece uppermost, pin, tack and machine stitch the denim to the needlepoint. The needle should run along the last line of stitching – check after the first 15cm (6in) that you have placed it correctly. The edge of the stitching should meet the denim exactly: too close, and you will not produce a crisp seam; too far away, and the canvas will show. Start and finish about 5cm (2in) in from the bottom corners, thus leaving a gap along the bottom edge.

3 Machine stitch again just around the corners, and then snip off the excess and fabric quite closely.

4 Turn right side out and ease out the corners, using a tapestry needle to pull them out gently if necessary.

5 Stuff the cushion with wadding, pushing it well into the corners, and slip stitch the gap closed by hand.

Cross stitch

Cross stitch is often used as an alternative to tent stitch and is enjoying something of a revival, probably engendered by the renewed popularity of the flower and fruit patterns that are associated with the Berlin Work of the turn of the century, which usually employed this stitch. This is cross stitch at its simplest, sewn over one thread of canvas in each direction, which makes it double the thickness of ordinary tent stitch and therefore well suited to soft-furnishing items made from canvas embroidery. However, cross stitch is not limited to this one form and can be worked in a number of different decorative versions, from double to oblong cross stitch, each useful for producing a specific finished effect.

working cross stitch

Cross stitch has two important attributes: its hardwearing finish, and the fact that it distorts the canvas very little, which can be especially useful if you are stitching a rug made up of squares that are to be sewn together. In addition, if you stitch with good tension there may be no distortion at all, and the piece will not need to be worked on a frame. The drawbacks to cross stitch are that it uses more wool and also takes longer to work than tent stitch. Cross stitch variations are numerous and can make interesting backgrounds for geometric patterns. They are also useful where added texture is required. With some forms of cross stitch the canvas shows through, intentionally, which creates an almost lacy effect.

Working the stitches

Cross stitch is worked in straight lines backwards and forwards across the canvas. Be sure to keep the top stitch of each cross facing in the same direction, otherwise the finished piece will look messy. In geometric and multi-stitch designs, the pattern may dictate that the top stitches face in different directions, but these changes are carefully planned and should be followed closely to ensure that the patterning is not confused by top stitches worked the wrong way round, as this results in an untidy-looking finish.

Stitches may be carried over more than one canvas thread as in long-armed cross stitch (fig 5 right), as in the surround to the Sampler on page 92, where they are worked over two threads in each direction.

Canvas gauge

Canvas gauge in relation to the yarn selected is an important consideration when using cross stitch, as four strands of wool will have to fit into each hole. If the holes are too small, and the stitches will be too tight creating a bumpy finish; too large, and the coverage will be insfficient, leaving the canvas showing between the stitches. For this reason too, cross stitch is best worked on a mono rather than double-thread (Penelope) canvas.

As a general rule, 10 gauge canvas works well with single-thread tapestry wool; the yarn can be doubled for working on a 7/8 canvas. Experimentation is useful if using stranded wools; stitch some small test pieces to find the number of strands that will suit your chosen canvas.

Cross stitch

The most usual method of working the crosses in needlepoint is to complete each cross stitch before starting the next one. All the top stitches should be lying in the same direction.

1 Make a tent stitch, bringing the needle up through the canvas and down diagonally above, to the left (fig 1).

2 Complete the cross by making a stitch that crosses the first one and lies in the opposite direction (fig 2).

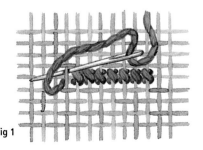

fig 1

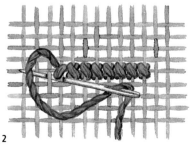

fig 2

Oblong cross stitch

This stitch is made in the same way as cross stitch (left) but the stitch is elongated, crossing more threads of canvas in one direction than the other (figs 3 and 4).

Oblong cross stitch may be worked in rows starting from the left or the right. Double oblong, is oblong cross stitch with an extra stitch made across the centre. The end result looks like lines of little haystacks.

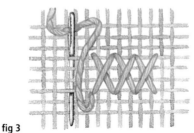

fig 3

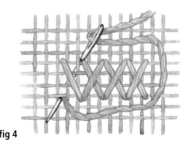

fig 4

Long-armed cross stitch

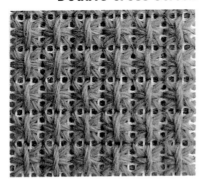

In this stitch, the stitches do not stand alone but are connected by the long arm, which stretches across into the adjacent stitch (figs 5 and 6).

Long-armed cross stitch must be worked in horizontal rows from left to right, starting each row anew. It should be used as a stitch on its own – or in a striped design – as it will not fit around or against other needlepoint stitches.

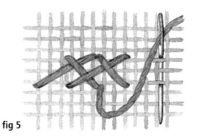

fig 5

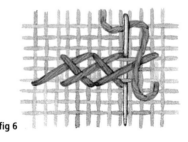

fig 6

Double cross stitch

Also known as Leviathan or Smyrna cross stitch, double cross stitch consists of a basic cross stitch as described left, with another cross made over the top in horizontal and vertical directions (figs 7 and 8).

In two colours, it produces a striking effect. The illustration shows it worked on a gauge whereby the canvas shows through, which can be decorative. Thicker yarn or a smaller gauge will give you more solid coverage.

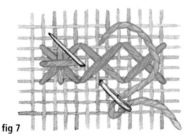

fig 7

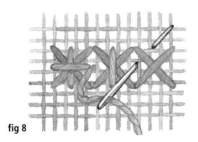

fig 8

art deco bag

This little bag displays art deco style at its most charming and was copied from an original 1930s design. The colours are bright but soft and are used straight, with no subtle shading or depth of tone; nevertheless, the finished effect is very sophisticated. The lining has been attached to the metal clasp with a clever little ruffle to cover what would otherwise be an ugly join, creating a pretty and unusual finishing touch.

It is essential that the stitched canvas pieces are not distorted, as the two sides would otherwise pull against one another and the gusset in different directions – even a small amount of distortion will spoil the finish. For this reason, cross stitch is the best choice.

About the bag

Approximate finished size:
15 x 17cm (6 x 6¾ in). The bag has been worked using Paterna Persian yarn.

You will need

For the needlepoint:
13-gauge interlock or mono de luxe
    canvas, 35 x 50cm (14⅜ x 20in)
Size 20 tapestry needle
Stranded wool in Paterna or Appletons
    colours shown in the key on page 55
For the bag:
Metal bag frame, 14cm (5½ in) across top
50 x 100cm (20 x 40in) co-ordinating silk
    or taffeta, for lining
Sewing thread to match fabric
Button thread (optional) for stitching the
    bag to the frame.

To work the needlepoint

The bag is worked in cross stitch carried over one thread of canvas.

Start at the top right-hand corner and build the pattern outwards. Work the cross stitch in rows either across or up and down, but do not mix the two directions. Make sure that all the top stitches run in the same direction. Use 1 strand of Paterna Persian yarn or 2 strands of Appletons crewel wool. Work 2 side pieces and 1 gusset piece, following chart on page 55.

To make up the bag

1 Block the completed canvas pieces and trim the unstitched margins to 1.5cm (½in) all round.
2 Using these pieces as templates, cut out the same 3 shapes in lining fabric.
3 Fold in each end margin of the canvas gusset and press.
4 With right sides together, pin and tack the canvas gusset around the curved edge of one canvas side of the bag, starting at the centre of the base and moving outwards in each direction. Machine stitch or backstitch along the seam. Sew in some of the stitched canvas around the curved base edges to smooth out the stepped curve in the embroidery. Cover all of the unstitched canvas. Clip into the canvas margin up to the seam every 2cm (¾in) to ease the canvas around the curved edge.
5 Repeat step 4 to sew the opposite side of the canvas gusset to the second canvas side of the bag.
6 Fold in the canvas margins at the top and along the sides. Press and tack.

7 Assemble the lining in the same way. Fold and press the seam allowances for ease of stitching. With the right side out, place the lining inside the bag. Hand stitch the lining to the bag around the top and sides and across the gusset.

8 To make the ruffle, cut out 2 strips of lining fabric, each 4 x 50cm (1½ x 20in). For each strip, fold under 1.5cm (½in) at each end and press. Fold the cut edges lengthways to the centre and press (fig 1). Fold the strip in half lengthways to hide the cut edges and press. Stitch a gathering thread along the centre of the strip (fig 2). Pull up to match the length around the open sides and top of one half of the bag.

9 Hand stitch the ruffle along the gathering seam to the edge of the lining (fig 3), so it protrudes from the edges.

10 Hand stitch the frame to the bag using buttonhole thread or doubled sewing thread, starting at the centre top and working outwards (fig 4).

fig 1

fig 2

fig 3

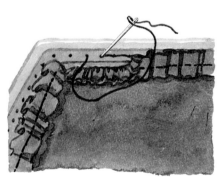

fig 4

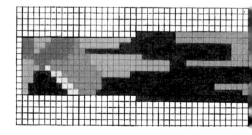

Stranded wool	Paterna	Appletons	skeins				
blue	553	564	2	black	220	993	3
grey	202	964	2	maroon	900	505	1
honey	734	472	2	deep pink	943	501A	1
				pale pink	933	942	1

bag side

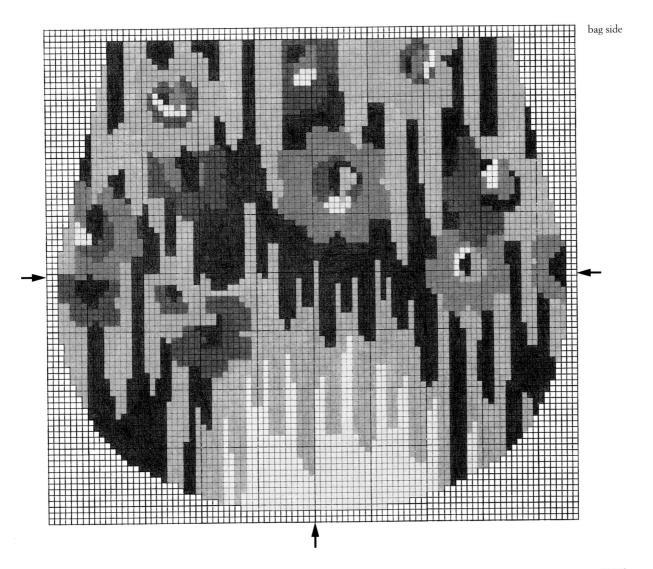

gusset

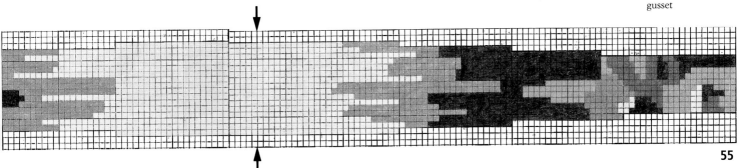

55

poppy slippers

The idea of stitching your own shoes or slippers can be very appealing. Although it is expensive to have them professionally made up, they should last many years and give a great deal of pleasure to the wearer.

With their big poppy heads on the toes, these slippers are decidedly feminine, but more masculine motifs can be used to transform them into an excellent gift for a man. The Victorians often stitched slippers with animal heads – particularly foxes – on the toes, or with monograms. Plaid patterns are also suitable, and are easy to draw out on graph paper before committing the design to canvas. Some pattern sizing is given to enable you to make a pair to fit; use the outlines as a template if creating your own design. The slippers may seem large, but they will make up smaller than you might expect.

About the slippers

Approximate finished size: the slippers shown are UK size 3. They have been stitched using Rowan tapestry wool.

You will need

For the needlepoint:
10-gauge interlock or mono de luxe canvas, approximately 38 x 50cm (15 x 20in)
Size 18 or 20 tapestry needle
Tapestry wool in the Rowan or Anchor colours shown in the key on page 59
For the slippers:
1 pair round-toed inner soles
Felt
Lining fabric
Binding, for top edge

To work the needlepoint

The design is worked in cross stitch carried over one thread of canvas.

Work the flowers and foliage first, and then stitch the background. Work the cross stitch in rows either across or up and down, but do not mix the two directions. Make sure that all the top stitches run in the same direction.

To make up the slippers

1 Block the completed canvas and trim the unstitched margin to approximately 2cm (¾in) all round. Use this as a template to cut 2 pieces of lining fabric.
2 Machine stitch canvas and lining together along the top edge of needlepoint stitches, leaving 1.5cm (⅝in) unstitched either side of centre back seam. Trim excess canvas and lining to within 6mm (¼in) of worked canvas.

3 With right sides together, pin and machine stitch the centre back seam on the needlepoint uppers. Trim and press seam open. Repeat, to stitch centre back seam on lining uppers. Complete stitching round top edge by hand.

4 Measure round the lower edge of the finished canvaswork upper and check that it is 3mm (⅛in) shorter than the outer edge of the inner sole. Using the inner sole as a template cut 4 pieces of felt to the same size.

5 Pin 2 felt soles together with an inner sole between. Fold under the canvas

round the lower edge of the upper; tack. Trim down unstitched canvas to 6mm (¼in). Fit the sole to base edge of the upper and, keeping the lining edge free carefully blanket stitch the canvas edge to the felt sole all round the outer edge spacing stitches 6mm (¼in) apart.

6 Starting at centre back, halve binding over the raw edges of canvas and lining. Turn under raw end of binding and overlap the opposite raw end to neaten. Hand stitch binding to slipper all round. Turn under the lower edge of lining and slip stitch to the felt inner sole.

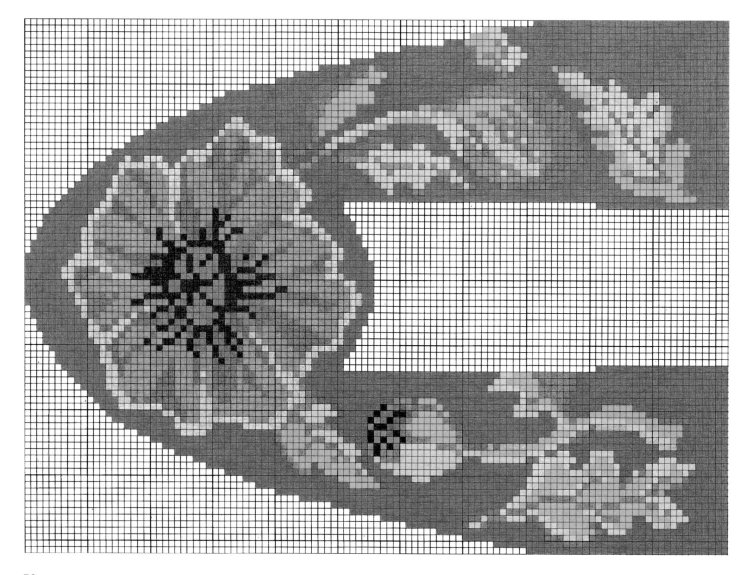

left slipper

Tapestry wool	Rowan	Anchor	skeins
pale orange	C20	8302	2
orange	C22	8232	3
terracotta	J412	8348	1
purple	K423	8528	1
aquamarine	P89	8918	3
emerald	P90	8938	2
bright green	T38	9102	2
charcoal	A625	9798	1
grey-blue	M88	8738	1
royal blue	N57	8692	9

Enlarging the slippers.
Measure round the outer edge of the inner sole
and lengthen the top edge of the upper to this
length minus 3mm (⅛in). Generally the top edge
of the upper will lengthen by approximately 7mm
(¼in) per size.

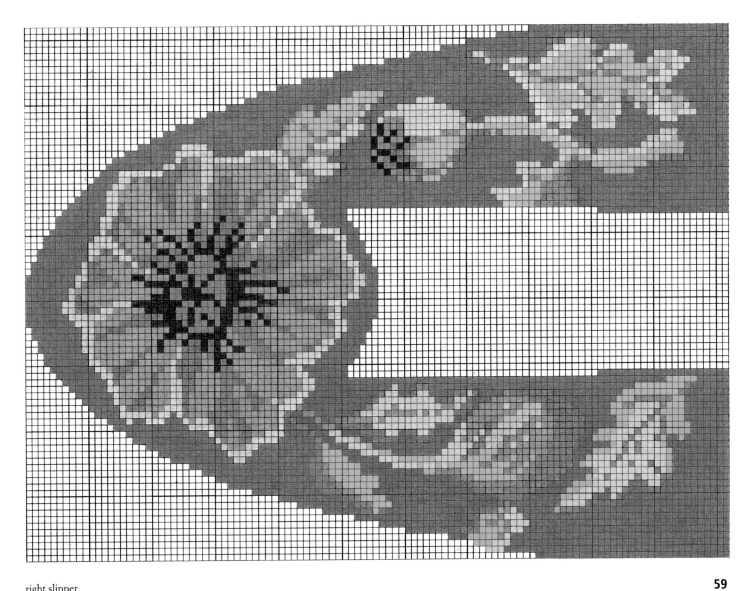

right slipper

Shading

Even in its simplest form, shading can give depth and life to what might otherwise be a flat, dull image. In wool needlepoint the matt yarn causes the colours to absorb rather than reflect light. Unless some shading is included, the result can be deadening if the design calls for any perspective.

There are a number of ways in which shading can be incorporated into a design without employing too many colours. For example, when observed closely, the shading on printed textiles and wallpapers may seem crude and the colours surprising, but the results are effective and often painterly. It is the density of the shades – the 'tone' – and their juxtaposition to other colours that is more important than the colours themselves. The same approach works well in needlepoint. However, one of the advantages of needlepoint is that no such restrictions apply and the stitcher is free to use as many colours as desired.

shading techniques

Although shading can be approached in numerous ways, the three simplest techniques are solid-block shading, which is used for most printed canvases; dotted shading, where the lines are blurred by dotting one colour into the next; and split-yarn shading, where yarns are mixed and stitched together. All are described below. The most obvious route to shading is to use closely graded colours that move almost imperceptibly from one shade to the next. Hand-painted canvases, which can be coloured with graded shades, are more widely available in the United States than in Europe and this method is therefore more common there. Manufacturers' shade cards are often organized into groups to accommodate this approach.

Solid-block shading

The choice of tones, or colour densities, is important when using this method of shading, in which solid blocks of colours are worked next to each other to give the effect of light and dark areas. This method demands a little artistic skill and judgement of colour. For example, the point at which a tablecloth falls from the table edge demands a dramatic change of depth in the colour to create the effect of perspective. However, casting a shadow on a petal in order to give it shape and curve usually requires a gentler change of tone, but not always from the same colour group. Looking at paintings shows us that white is often shaded not with grey but with purple, green or other unexpected hues. The same technique can be applied successfully to needlepoint.

1 Use an ordinary (not coloured) pencil to sketch the shapes roughly and shade them in until you achieve the desired effect. The depth of tone will be shown by the depth of the shading, which will assist you in choosing colours.

2 Stitch the motifs bit by bit, starting with a piece in the main colour and then shading it as you go along, in order to build up the picture gradually. Do not stitch all of one colour first and then all of the next, and so on.

Dotting

This method of shading consists of mixing one shade into the next by stitching dots of a darker shade into a lighter shade (or vice versa), resulting in a gradual change of colour rather than a distinct line between the two different shades. It is especially effective where you need to move quickly from very dark to very light tones across a piece of needlepoint. This can be done with any yarn, and can be used to good effect to enhance printed canvas designs.

1 Stitch the area of the first colour, and then work random stitches of the same colour in the canvas still to be worked.
2 Take the second colour – which can be dramatically different from the first– and stitch around these dots. Then work dots of this colour in the next area of unstitched canvas.
3 Fill in around the dots with a third colour, and so on.

Split-yarn shading

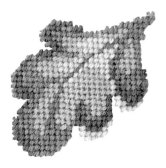

This method involves mixing colours to create a graded colour change. On smaller-gauge canvases this can only be done with fine or stranded yarns that can be split and mixed, and then threaded together on the needle. On 7/8 gauge canvas, two strands of single-thread tapestry wool can be used. Depending upon the number of threads required to cover the canvas, the new shade can be added strand by strand until a solid colour is achieved. Choose shades that are close to one another, and use short lengths only. For example, using three-stranded wool:

1 Begin stitching with all three strands of the first colour.
2 When you wish to start shading, change one strand to the next shade and continue stitching.
3 Next, change two strands to the next shade, and continue stitching.

4 Finally, change all three strands to the next shade, and continue stitching in the new shade.

You have moved from one colour to the next in several stages. To move through a larger range, omit step 4 and introduce a third shade, and so on.

needlepoint bow

Decorative bows are often used in home furnishings to add interest on picture hangers or caught above a curtain arrangement, perhaps to hold a sprig of sweet-smelling lavender. This bow is worked in tent stitch following the colours on a length of ribbon. To echo the feel of a ribbon bow, dotted shading is used to add depth to the twists in the ribbon knot and folds in the bow loops, producing a three-dimensional effect.

About the bow
Approximate finished size: 22cm (9in).
The bow has been stitched using Paterna Persian yarn.

You will need
For the needlepoint:
10-gauge interlock or mono de luxe
   canvas, 30 x 38cm (12 x 15in)
Size 18 or 20 tapestry needle
Stranded wool in the Paterna or DMC
   Medici wool in the colours shown in
   the key below.

For lining the bow:
25 x 30cm (10 x 12in) toning silk dupion
Matching sewing thread
1.5cm (½in) diameter curtain ring

To work the needlepoint
The design is worked in tent stitch, and the diagonal method is recommended.
   Start stitching at the centre and work outwards. Work the brown dotted shading before filling in the khaki behind it. Use 2 strands of either Paterna Persian yarn or DMC Medici wool throughout.

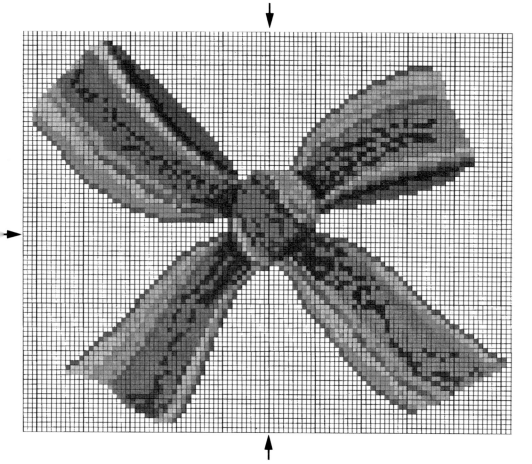

Stranded wool	Paterna	DMC Medici	skeins
khaki	453	8501	2
brown	452	8610	1
dark brown	450	8500	1
light turquoise	583	8996	1
bright turquoise	582	8995	1
dark turquoise	580	8993	1
sugar pink	963	8151	1
hot pink	962	8153	1
deep pink	961	8155	1

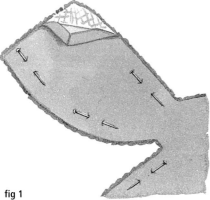

fig 1

To line the bow

1 Trim the canvas around the completed bow, leaving a 1cm (⅜in) unstitched margin all round.

2 Cut out the silk dupion lining fabric to the same shape and size as the bow.

3 Turn under the cut edges of the canvas, snipping into the margin as necessary to make it lie flat; tack.

4 Place the bow face down on a flat surface and pin on the lining fabric. Turn under the cut edges of the lining to match the outer edges of the bow (fig 1), snip into the margins as before. Slip stitch the lining to the bow all round.

5 To form a hanger, hand stitch the curtain ring to the wrong side of the bow behind the knot.

patchwork stool top

Using blocks of light or bright colours alongside dark or muted tones can bend the eye's perception and create perspective where none really exists. You need to look closely to see how the colours have been placed to manipulate the light. This deceptively simple but clever shading technique is often used in patchwork, and the design here is taken from the famous 'log cabin' patchwork pattern. If you plan to substitute colours to fit a different scheme, it is essential that shades of equal tone (depth of colour) are chosen to maintain the effect.

About the stool top

Approximate design size: 31.5 x 41cm (12½ x 16⅜in). The stool top has been stitched using DMC tapestry wool.

You will need

For the needlepoint:
10-gauge double-thread (Penelope) canvas, 43 x 54cm (17 x 21in)
Size 18 or 20 tapestry needle
Tapestry wool in the DMC or Anchor colours shown in the key on page 68
For the stool:
Stool with pad 31.5 x 41cm (12½ x 16⅜in)
60cm (24in) of furnishing cotton, 115cm (45in) wide
Matching sewing thread
1.7m (2yd) No 4 piping cord

To work the needlepoint

The design is worked in tent stitch, the continental method is recommended.

Stitch the pattern square by square, starting at the top right-hand corner. It is important to work all the stitches in the same direction. This means that on the downward strips of colour, stitches are put in side by side. Do not turn the work around to stitch in downward lines, as this will create unevenness and the work may pucker.

Tapestry wool	DMC	Anchor	skeins
dark red	7138	8442	4
salmon pink	7136	8438	2
medium pink	7153	8488	3
light pink	7605	8452	3
pale pink	7132	8394	2
dark violet	7242	8594	1
medium violet	7243	8590	4
lilac	7896	8524	4
petrol grey	7295	8738	2
navy blue	7823	8694	2
turquoise blue	7995	8808	3
light blue	7813	8806	2
pale blue	7301	8814	2
bright yellow	7742	8120	2
pale yellow	7727	8016	2
green	7956	8966	2

To make up the stool cover

1 Block the completed canvas and trim the unstitched margin to approximately 2cm (¾ in) all round.

2 Measure round the needlepoint and make up a length of covered piping cord to this length plus 7cm (3in). Lay the piping on the right side of the needlepoint following step 6 of the instructions for the Circus Cushion on page 28. Pin, tack and machine stitch around the needlepoint. Hand stitch ends together neatly to fit.

3 Place the needlepoint on top of the stool and measure from the top down to the chosen length. Measure all round the needlepoint top. Cut out 1 piece of fabric to the top circumference measurement plus a 2cm (¾in) seam allowance by the chosen length plus 3.5cm (1½in) for seam and hem.

4 Pin, tack and machine stitch the fabric piece together to form a ring, taking a 1cm (⅜in) seam allowance. Neaten and press the seam open. Turn under a double 1cm (⅜in) hem all round the lower edge; pin and stitch.

5 With right sides together and the seam positioned centrally in one long side, pin and tack the side piece to the needlepoint. The piping will be caught in between. Using a piping foot, machine stitch around the edge, keeping close to the piping. Turn the cover right side out. Slide the needlepoint cover over the stool top.

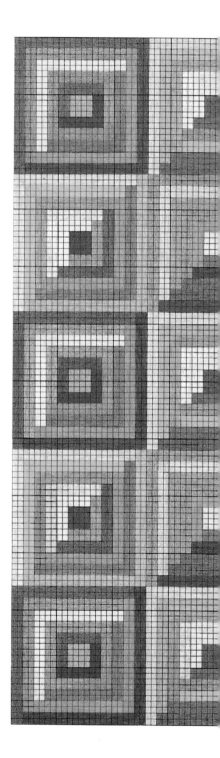

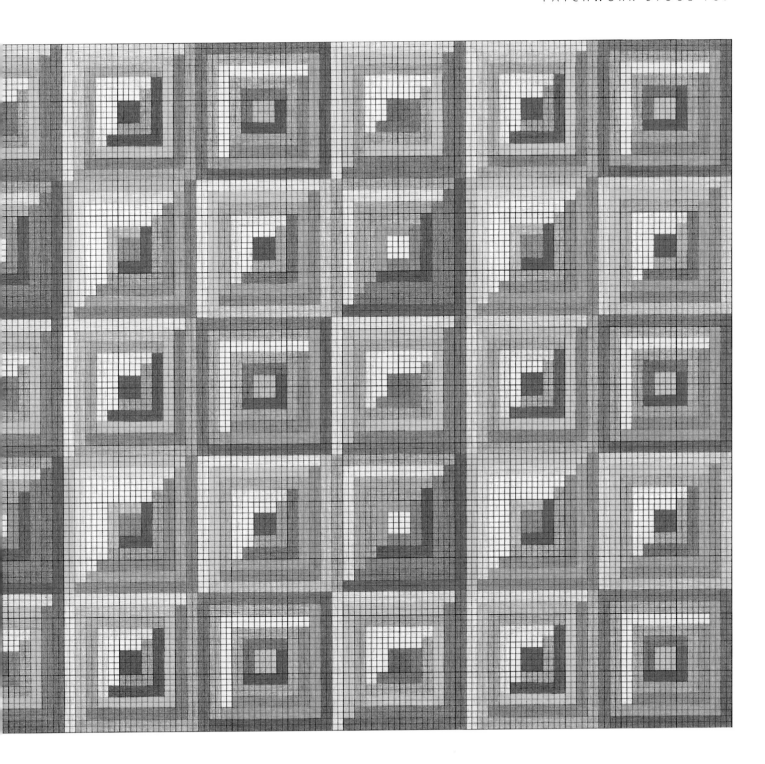

cherub cushion

A classical theme of perching cherubs holding fruits and ribbons makes an appealing design for a cushion that would sit well in a period drawing room. The colours are soft and subtle, and the shading of the cherubs is worth studying. Note how daring the off-white highlights are – they are not closely graded to the adjacent colours, but are bold and strong. However, the beiges and browns depicting the darker areas are dotted into one another, making the move from one colour to the next almost imperceptible. Note, too, how the eyes and mouths are simply suggested with one or two stitches.

fig 1

About the cushion

Approximate finished size: 45 x 22cm (18 x 9 in). The cushion has been stitched using Appletons tapestry wool.

You will need

For the needlepoint:
12-gauge Interlock or mono de luxe canvas, 60 x 36cm (24 x 14¾in)
Size 20 tapestry needle
Tapestry wool in the Appletons or Anchor colours shown in the key on pages 72 and 73
For the cushion:
50cm (20in) square medium-weight furnishing cotton
38cm (15in) matching zip
Sewing thread to match fabric
1.6m (1¾yd) ruffle trim
50 x 28cm (20 x 11in) cushion pad

To work the needlepoint

The design is worked in tent stitch, the diagonal method is recommended.

Start with the cherubs and other features, then stitch the background starting at the top right hand corner and work diagonally across the canvas.

To make up the cushion

1 Block the completed canvas and trim the unstitched margin to approximately 2cm (¾in) all round.
2 Pin and tack the ruffle trim to the canvas front of the cushion cover, gathering the corners to ensure that they will fan out around the curve when the cover is truned to the right side (fig 1).
3 Cut out 2 pieces of backing fabric, 50 x 20cm (20 x 8in) and 50 x 10cm (20 x 4in). Insert the zip between these 2 pieces, following steps 3 and 4 of the Circus Cushion on page 26.
4 With right sides together, pin, tack and machine stitch the cushion back to the front, sandwiching the ruffle trim in between. For each seam, the needle should run along the last line of stitching, so that no canvas shows and the seam does not encroach on the embroidery. Machine stitch again just around the corners, and then snip off the excess canvas and fabric quite closely.
5 Turn the cover right side out and ease out the corners, using a tapestry needle to pull them out gently if necessary. Insert the cushion pad and close the zip.

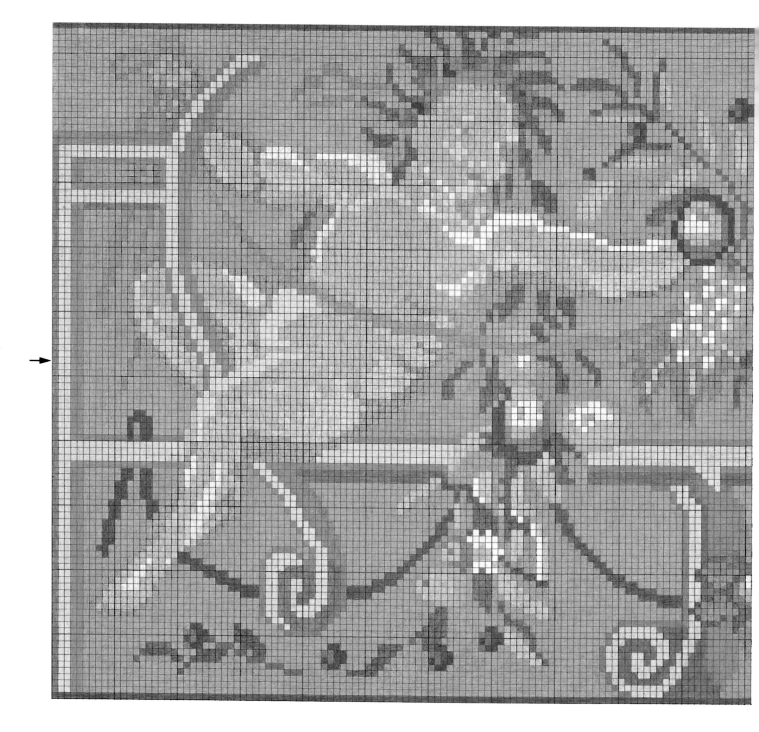

Tapestry wool	Appletons	Anchor	skeins									
▪ dark green	356	7198	2	▪ dusky green	292	9066	2	▪ pale yellow	692	8054	3
▪ mid green	355	9176	1	▪ dark olive	344	9216	1	▪ light brown	762	9326	1
▪ light green	342	9054	1	▪ olive green	333	9306	1	▪ pale brown	761	9324	1
				▪ very pale green	691	9046	1	▪ grey-brown	751	9402	1

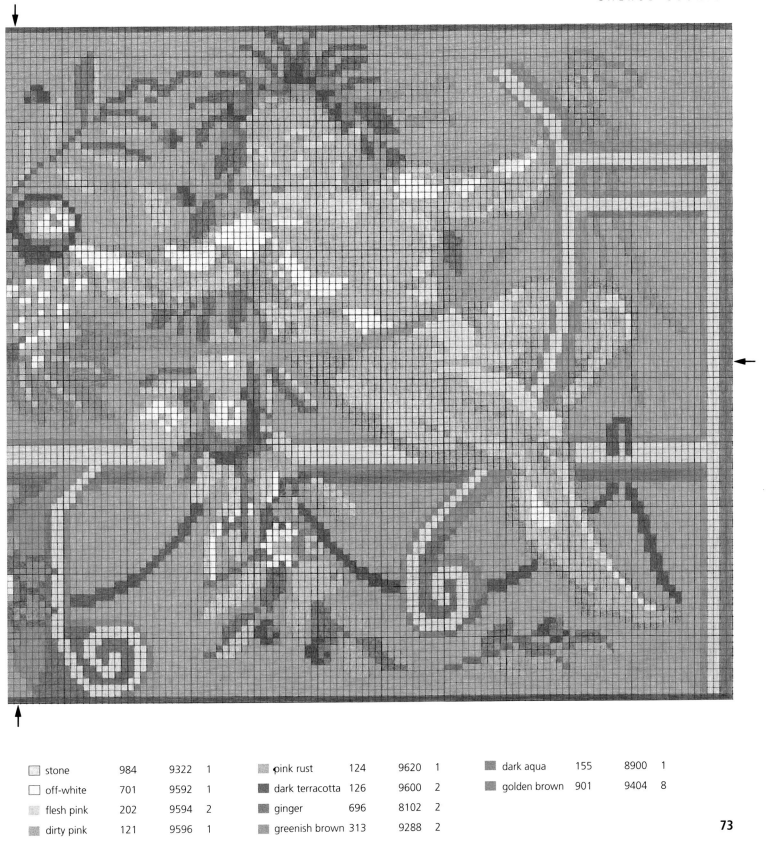

	stone	984	9322	1		pink rust	124	9620	1		dark aqua	155	8900	1
	off-white	701	9592	1		dark terracotta	126	9600	2		golden brown	901	9404	8
	flesh pink	202	9594	2		ginger	696	8102	2					
	dirty pink	121	9596	1		greenish brown	313	9288	2					

73

Stitch patterns

Although most needlepoint is executed in tent stitch, this is by no means the end of the story. Possibilities for stitch combinations and pattern varieties are endless – textured stitches can be worked on top of smoother stitches, patterns can be made to overlap and interlock, and the use of different canvas gauges, thread types and colour combinations can add further dimensions to the visual effects.

An inventive stitcher may create his or her own stitch patterns to fit a particular purpose. These fancy stitches are rarely suitable for figurative work, but can be used to excellent effect as borders and backgrounds, or as patterns in their own right. Stitching some experimental pieces is well worth the effort in order to keep a record of patterns. Such records are the origins of the traditional sampler.

long stitch

Long, straight stitches are easy and quick to make, and long-stitch methods fall into two distinct working techniques. The first is freestyle and may be used to replace the more usual tent stitch where large areas of canvas need to be covered, in wall hangings for example or in simple easy-to-stitch projects. The second technique is where the stitches are counted to form repeating geometric colour patterns worked over regular numbers of threads. This is commonly used where needlepoint is employed in the manner of a furnishing fabric, as opposed to pictorially.

In the seventeenth century, bed curtains were often worked in long stitch, sometimes with sets of chair seat covers to match. Long stitches of both methods have the advantage of not pulling the canvas out of shape, but using a frame is strongly recommended to ensure an even tension that will result in a flat canvas.

Freestyle long stitch

Freestyle long stitch for small pictures is straightforward to work. The shapes can be filled in with stitches of the required length, and even awkward shapes can be accommodated. If the work is to be framed, single stitches may be as long as necessary, although the longer they are the less well they cover the canvas. Doubling the yarn or working very long stitches twice over may be sufficient to overcome this, so a little experimentation is worthwhile.

For more ambitious pieces, long stitch can be artistically challenging where light and shade, perspective and texture are called for. It is the nearest that needlepoint gets to painting and is currently enjoying popularity. Colours may be mixed on the needle to add highlights or split-yarn shading (see page 63), or to alleviate the flatness of large areas of single-colour stitching.

Stitches should not be made that are too long as they may work loose or snag with use. The length and placement of stitches can also be used to add pattern and textural interest, a technique that requires practice to feel comfortable with as there are no set rules to follow.

Neither printed canvases nor charts can show every nuance of shade and stitch length that goes into such designs.

Long stitch used in a straigtforward manner to fill in areas of colour.

Long stitch using mixed colours and varying stitch lengths to create shading and texture.

bargello

Geometric, counted long-stitch patterns are commonly called Bargello work, although strictly speaking the term applies only to the flame-stitch pattern that is associated with the Palazzo Bargello Museum in Florence, Italy, where four seventeenth-century chairs are worked in a repeating wave formation which is why this is called Florentine work. Traditionally, the bands of patterning are worked in graduated shading from dark to light using one colour at a time. This is demonstrated in the Bargello Bolster on page 78, where the repeating pattern consists of five bands of colour, each containing five graded shades. Silk threads are often used for highlights in Bargello work, but in old pieces the silk has often disappeared; it is now known that silk and wool 'argue' which causes the silk to disintegrate. As silk threads take a long time to disintergrate this should not deter you from using both threads in one piece of work.

Counted long-stitch patterns

Moving away from traditional Bargello style, endless combinations of geometric counted-thread patterns are possible, from interlocking rectangles and diamonds to cleverly shaded stitch formations that trick the eye to suggest tumbling blocks or woven threads.

Straight, long stitches are quick to make, and designs consisting of simply shaped, solid blocks of colour may be stitched using long stitch in place of the usual tent stitch. The stitches may be even and counted, or randomly stitched to fill an irregular shape. Working in this way takes some practice. Spectacular effects with shading can be achieved by threading two colours together onto the needle. Short stitches are suitable for a wide variety of uses, but long stitches are only suitable for use on items like pictures or wall hangings where the threads will not wear or snag.

Straightforward Bargello style counted thread stitching in a traditional wave pattern.

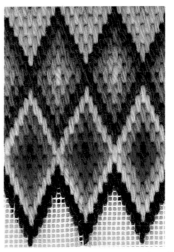

A variation on Bargello counted thread stitching creating interlocking diamonds.

Bargello bolster

This bolster employs one of the simplest of Bargello patterns, with all the stitches carried over the same number of threads. This particular one was stitched by an elderly lady, who bought up bags of threads in the Harrods' sale every year, and had a natural aptitude for putting them together. The colours are numerous and daring and not every repeat in the original is exactly the same. When a colour has run out, she has used the closest she could find in her workbasket, but she has instinctively used the graded colour technique that is typical of the genre.

About the bolster

Approximate finished design size: 40 x 50cm (16 x 20in). The bolster was worked with scrap wools, so the brand is not known. A successful choice of colours is simple to make: select 5 graded shades of each colour and put a line of black between each band.

You will need

For the needlepoint:
13-gauge interlock or mono de luxe canvas, 55 x 65cm (22 x 26in)
Size 20 or 22 tapestry needle
Tapestry wool in the Anchor or DMC colours shown in the key on page 81
For the bolster:
Two 53 x 10cm (21½ x 4in) pieces toning fabric
Matching sewing thread
45cm (18in) pad, 18cm (7in) in diameter
2 large buttons
1.2m (1¼yd) No 5 piping cord
For handmade buttons (optional):
1.2m (1¼yd) No 3 piping cord

fig 1

To work the needlepoint

The design is worked in long stitch carried over 2 threads of canvas. Take care not to stitch tightly; a frame is recommended.

Starting at the top, stitch the pattern row by row, beginning with a black one. Count the first row carefully and the rest should fall into place.

Always bring the needle up through the canvas below the work (in an empty hole), and push it down to join the bottom of the row above. This will create an even finish and smooth stitches.

fig 2

It is important that the stitches cover the canvas well or holes will show when it is wrapped around the bolster pad, spoiling the finished look.

To make up the bolster

1 Block the completed canvas well to make it as square as possible, usually long stitch stays quite straight, making it a good choice for this project.
2 Cut the end fabric in half lengthways to create 2 strips.
3 Make a length of piping following step 5 of the instructions for the Circus Cushion on page 26. Stitch the piping along the 2 longer edges of the stitched canvas, following step 3 of the instructions for the Strawberry Album Cover on page 30. Place the 2 strips of fabric over the piping and pin in place, tack and machine stitch to secure.
4 Run 2 lines of gathering thread evenly along the cut edge of the fabric at both ends (fig 1).
5 Fold the needlepoint in half, with right sides facing. Tack the edges of the canvas together, taking care that the edges of the stitching meet as exactly as possible. Tack the fabric edges together, to form a long tube with fabric ends. Machine stitch along the tacked seam.
6 Turn the tube right side out and ease the pad inside the tube.
7 Pull up the gathering threads on the end pieces as tightly as possible and hand stitch across the gathering with big stitches to hold it firmly in place (fig 2).
8 Hand stitch the buttons in place at each end of the bolster to cover the gathered cut edges.

fig 3

To make handmade buttons (optional)
This is not recommended for the inexperienced sewer.

1 Make up 2 strips of piping approximately 40cm (16in) long. Pull up the cord a little to curve the piping naturally.

2 Snip the fabric every 1cm (⅜in) or so up to the seam (fig 3).

3 Wind each length of piping in a circular fashion to make a Catherine-wheel shape, with the cut edges splaying outwards. Hand stitch the piping together as you go.

4 When each wheel is a suitable size, tuck the end underneath and snip off the piping. Trim off excess fabric from underneath.

5 Flatten each wheel using a hot steam iron. Tuck the cut edges underneath and flatten again. Turn over and flatten the finished button again.

6 Hand stitch the buttons on to the ends of the bolster.

Tapestry wool		Anchor	DMC	skeins
■	black	9800	7309	3
■	olive	9068	7377	1
■	forest green	9028	7387	1
■	fir-tree green	9078	7396	1
■	apple green	9094	7382	1
□	pale green	9058	7400	1
■	damask rose	8354	7139	1
■	rust	9602	7212	1
■	rose pink	8400	7205	1
■	salmon pink	8306	7760	1
■	pale salmon	8364	7761	1
■	dark brown	9622	7468	1
■	dark gold	8024	7474	1
■	old gold	8020	7484	1
■	greeny yellow	9284	7679	1
□	pale yellow	9192	7501	1
■	royal purple	8530	7259	1
■	deep purple	8528	7257	1
■	mid purple	8526	7255	1
■	lilac	8524	7253	1
■	mauve	8522	7896	1
■	navy blue	8742	7319	1
■	grey blue	8738	7593	1
■	dusky blue	8788	7313	1
■	light blue	8814	7301	1
□	pale blue	8714	7284	1

chair seat

This charming pattern is made up of oval repeating shapes, and combines tent stitch with a Bargello-style surround. It is eminently suitable for chair coverings, cushions, pelmets and many other furnishing items. However, for dining chairs that are used every day you may wish to change the long stitches to tent stitch for extra durability.

In this particular piece, which is around 100 years old, the tent-stitch areas have been worked in silk, with the long stitches in crewel wool, and the canvas is a soft linen that is rarely found nowadays. Whoever stitched the piece had good tension, for the stitching has caused little distortion to the very soft canvas base.

About the chair seat

Measure your chair to find the design size. The canvas used here is an antique 20-gauge linen canvas. However, since this is extremely fine, difficult to obtain and too small a gauge for most needlepoint yarns, 18-gauge interlock canvas is a good substitute. You may, however, choose to stitch this design on a much larger scale.

You will need

For the needlepoint:
Canvas of your choice, at least 6cm (2½in) larger than finished piece all round
Tapestry needle in size to suit gauge of canvas chosen
Stranded wools and cottons in the colours shown in the key on page 84
For the template:
Square of calico or sheeting, 5cm (2in) larger than finished template all round
Waterproof marker pen

To work the needlepoint

1 Make up a template of the seat area (see right) and mark out this shape centrally on the canvas.
2 Start by working the top line of long-stitch patterning that frames the top of the tent stitch roundels.
3 Next work the 4 lines of long stitch patterning below the roundels.
4 Stitch the flower motifs and their backgrounds in tent stitch - the diagonal or half cross-stitch methods are recommended.
5 Repeat step 2.
6 Work the gold long-stitch pattern that fills the gap created by the oval shapes.

To make the template

1 Fold the template fabric in half and mark lightly along the crease. Fold it in half the other way and mark along the crease, then fold and mark it diagonally in both directions. This will assist you in placing the fabric centrally.
2 Find the centre of the chair seat by measuring diagonally across it in both directions, and then place the fabric centrally on it. Stab a few pins into the seat to hold the fabric. If the seat has a drop front, back and sides, mark on the fabric where it folds under, as these will need to be cut out on the template.
3 Mark the fabric where the upholstery joins the wood, remove from the chair.
4 Cut out the fabric along the marked lines to form the template.

To make the chair seat

The pattern can be repeated endlessly, and will need to be placed centrally on a template of the item into which it is to be made. An upholsterer can make you a template, or you can make your own, as shown on page 82. If the seat needs re-upholstering, have it done before making the template, as this may alter the size and shape considerably.

Alternatively, where the upholstery joins the wood the stitched canvas can be cut to shape, glued and machine stitched to prevent fraying, tacked down and covered with gimp trim. You can thus stitch a piece of canvas that is larger all the round than the chair seat and let the upholsterer trim it to size.

Stranded wool		Appletons	DMC Medici
	deep pink	227	8114
	terracotta	126	8168
	light terracotta	206	8166
	flesh pink	122	8164
	dark green	647	8415
	leaf green	294	8414
	light green	292	8413
	pale green	352	8405
	dark gold	696	8303
	gold	694	8304
	light gold	692	8313

Stranded cotton		Anchor	DMC
	putty	830	822
	dark green	246	319
	light green	261	368
	dark blue	851	931
	light blue	1038	828
	terracotta	1015	347
	pale pink	1012	948

stitch variations

Stitches other than tent or cross stitch are useful for speed if large areas need to be covered, and they can also assist in ensuring that the piece keeps its shape. Some will fit around tent-stitch features, although slight adjustments may need to be made to the stitch lengths. Many stitches are less accommodating and are used in more precisely defined areas. Most of the stitches and stitch combinations here are straightforward if approached step by step and they can give a piece a textural dimension to create a professional finish.

Rhodes stitch

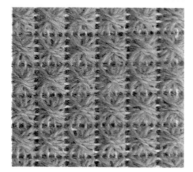

This is a raised filling stitch which covers squares of canvas. It is worked over four threads (using five holes) in each direction. Bring the needle up at A and down at B, up at C and down at D, and so on (fig 1). The final stitch is a full diagonal from one corner to the other (fig 2).

fig 1

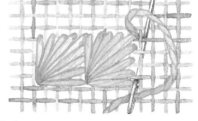

fig 2

Fan stitch

This stitch consists of nine straight stitches fanning out from a single hole to create a square, worked over four threads (figs 3 and 4).

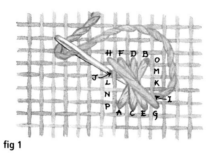

fig 3

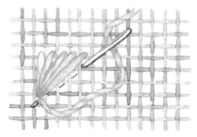

fig 4

Star stitch

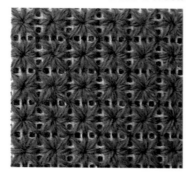

Star stitch is constructed with eight straight stitches radiating out from a central point (fig 5). Stitches can be made over two canvas threads (fig 6), or three if preferred.

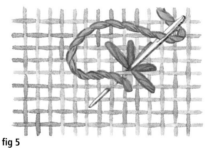

fig 5

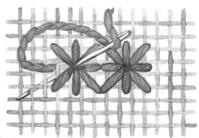

fig 6

Gobelin filling stitch

This is a useful alternative to tent stitch for large backgrounds. The number of threads it is worked over can be adjusted to suit the application. The stitches are worked in interlocking rows (fig 7). Bring the needle up through the canvas below the previous row (in an empty hole), and take it down between the stitches of the previous row (fig 8). There are many different versions of Gobelin stitch, each one based on straight stitches arranged in various directions to cover large areas of canvas. A combination of colours can be used to add another dimension to a stitched piece.

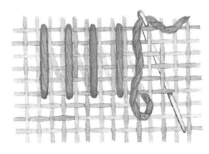

fig 7

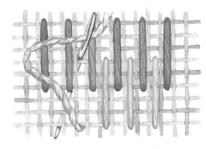

fig 8

Milanese stitch

The triangular pattern consists of four stitches of graded length, set in diagonal rows pointing in opposite directions (fig 9). The stitches are constructed in the same way as satin stitch and the triangles are stitched one at a time, working diagonally across the canvas and back (fig 10).

fig 9

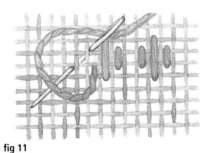

fig 10

Hungarian stitch

This stitch consists of rows of vertical stitches worked in repeating sets of stitches made over two, four and two canvas threads (fig 11). Each row is worked to fit into the preceding one. Stitching alternate rows in a second colour will add an interesting textured effect (fig 12).

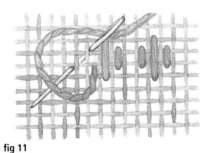

fig 11

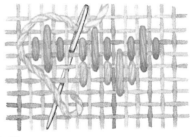

fig 12

evening purse

This simple-to-make but very effective purse uses a stitch pattern which prevents the finished canvas being pulled out of shape. The pattern for this piece is made up of squares of stitches intentionally facing in different directions in a planned formation. The first square is worked with the stitches starting from the top left-hand corner, the adjacent squares are stitched starting from the top right-hand corner, and so on, creating a subtle chequerboard effect as the light falls on the different directions of the stitched squares, and this is further emphasized by the sheen of the stranded cotton used for the projects. The beads are added at the end as a finishing touch.

About the purse

Approximate finished size: 20 x 14cm (8 x 5½in). The purse has been stitched using Anchor stranded cottons.

You will need

For the needlepoint:
14-gauge interlock or mono de luxe canvas, 30 x 45cm (12 x 18in)
Size 22 tapestry needle
Stranded cottons in the Anchor or DMC colours shown in the key on page 91
Fine sewing needle, to fit through your chosen beads
Strong gold sewing thread
320 small gold-tinted glass beads
For the purse:
38 x 20cm (15 x 8in) quilt padding
43 x 24cm (17 x 9½in) lining fabric
Matching sewing thread
Large press stud and strong sewing thread (optional)

To work the needlepoint

This pattern is best worked using diagonal tent stitch and is a good piece on which to start if you are unfamiliar with this method of stitching.

Work the squares first, starting at the top and working one square at a time, until the piece consists of 8 x 16 squares and measures 20 x 40cm (8 x 16in). Each square is 12 x 12 stitches.

Add the border, starting with 2 rows of oblong cross stitch, followed by an interlocking long-stitch pattern. When working the long stitch, try to ensure that the threads lie flat, not twisted, across the canvas.

Finish with 2 rows of tent stitch, worked in alternate directions to keep the canvas straight. Fill the corners with Rhodes stitch as shown on page 86.

Use 6 strands of embroidery cotton throughout.

To work the embroidery and beading

The flowers are embroidered on top of the points where 4 squares meet on the front section of the purse. Stitch the red buds first, using long stitch (fig 1). The 2 leaves are lazy daisy stitches (fig 2), and the stalks are 3 small stem stitches (fig 3). Flowers are not stitched on to the back section of the purse, but beads are placed where the squares of stitching intersect.

The beads are sewn on using backstitch, which helps to prevent them hanging loose. Bring the needle and thread up through the canvas, thread on the bead and then complete the stitch. Keep all the stitches facing in the same direction, so that the beads lie evenly. On the border, beads are sewn on between every other cross stitch. On the flowers, beads are sewn on leaf tips and buds.

To make up the purse

1 With right sides together and the canvas uppermost, machine stitch the lining to the stitched canvas, leaving a gap of 15cm (6in) along one of the shorter sides. The needle should run along the centre of the holes containing the last line of stitching for the front flap. For the rest of the bag, stitch along the first row of empty canvas. Experiment along one side first to check that the stitches are correctly aligned.

2 Trim the canvas and lining to 1cm (⅜in) all round and snip across the corners to ensure a crisp finish.

3 Turn the purse right side out and gently ease out the corners using a tapestry needle.

4 Push the quilt padding in through the opening and flatten it out inside the purse. Slip stitch the opening closed.

5 Fold up approximately 12cm (5in) of the front section. Using gold stranded cotton and a tapestry needle, oversew the edges together, stitching into the holes of the canvas.

6 To attach a fastener, use strong sewing thread and a sharp needle to sew a press stud on to the inside flap and to a matching point on the front of the purse. Sew carefully between the stitches.

NB To adjust the size of the finished piece, increase the number of stitches in each square. Alternatively, you can add more squares, but the width must be made up of an even number of squares in order to accommodate the surface embroidery of flowers and beads.

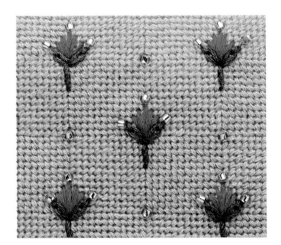

fig 1

fig 2

fig 3

Stranded cotton	Anchor	DMC	skeins
gold	363	976	23*
dark red	1005	815	1
dark green	224	500	1

* 1 skein is sufficient to stitch 7 squares of 12 x 12 stitches

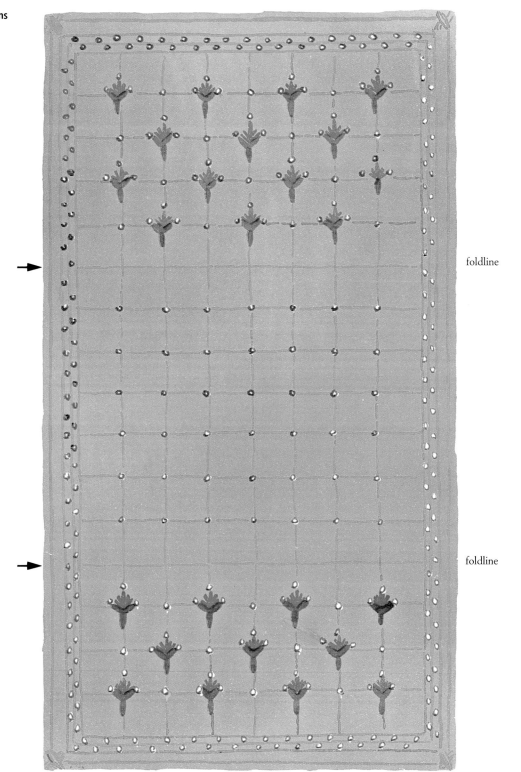

foldline

foldline

sampler

This stitch sampler employs 36 stitch combinations, each contained inside a square with 25 holes (24 threads) in each direction. The challenge is to make these stitch patterns fit together with some semblance of order. Note, too, how the stitch patterns and colour combinations have been chosen to balance out the whole design. Stitching a sampler undoubtedly engenders familiarity with the disciplines and restrictions that stitch combinations impose and from this, inventiveness can spring.

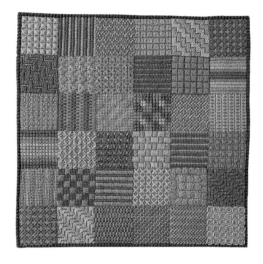

Stranded wool		Paterna	Appletons	skeins
	pale blue	213	875	3
	grey	506	561	3
	bright blue	554	462	3
	steel blue	504	743	3
	dark blue	502	746	1

About the sampler

Approximate design size: 27.5cm (10¾in) square. The sampler has been worked using Paterna Persian wool.

You will need

14-gauge interlock or mono de luxe
    canvas, 50cm (20in) square
Size 20 tapestry needle
Stranded wool in the Paterna or
    Appletons colours shown in the key

To work the needlepoint

It is important to count out the patterns on a piece of graph paper before committing them to canvas – it is very frustrating to find out later that the stitches will not fit evenly into the designated space. For this reason, it is also a good idea to work a stitch-patterned or geometric border before stitching the centre, to ensure that it fits: one or two stitches out, and a lot of unpicking may be required. Sometimes a little 'cheating' is necessary in order to achieve a fit, and there is no harm in this so long as it is done sensibly.

This design is also suitable for a cushion, but two or three rows of tent stitch in the darkest shade should be added around the edge so that it can be made up without spoiling the stitching.

Use the layout plan on page 96 as a guide to which stitch to use in each square. Mark the centre of the canvas and work the squares one at a time, starting with the 4 central squares and working outwards.

The layout plan on page 96 is also a guide to the number of canvas threads over which each stitch has been worked.

To finish

Block the completed canvas before framing. Do not trim, because the framer will need a good margin of canvas to wrap around the backing board.

To make the sampler into a cushion, follow the instructions for making up the Circus Cushion on pages 26 and 28.

Working the patterns Eight of the thirty six stitch combinations are illustrated with diagrams, the remaining twenty-eight are only summarily described.

3 Straight stitch and tent stitch combination

Work the straight stitches first, and then fill in the tent sttiches. Note how the tent stitches face in different directions to create chevron shapes.

6 Upright cross stitch, doubled

Start with a cross stitch made over 4 threads and worked horizontally and vertically. A second stitch is worked over the top, over 2 threads, in the more usual diagonal formation.

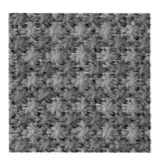

8 Christmas tree stitch on tent stitch

Work the tent stitch background first, taking care to angle the stitches as illustrated. This is important for creating the symmetry required for stitching the Christmas trees on the top.

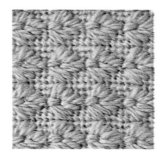

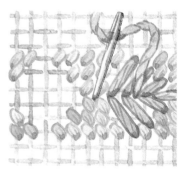

9 Rice stitch

This stitch is made up of large cross stitches worked over 4 threads with diagonal stitches worked over the arms of the cross stitches, over 2 threads.

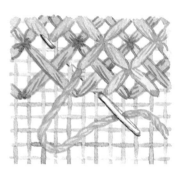

10 Fly stitch

Fly stitch is like chain stitch but with an open rather than a closed end. Here the stitches are worked close together and with a short anchoring stitch. In square no 35 they are spaced out, leaving an empty hole between the stitches and with long anchoring stitches that adjoin.

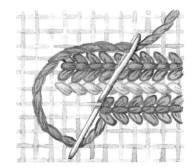

15 Tent stitch with French knots

This pattern consists of 4 stitch squares of tent stitch with French knots at the corners. To make a French knot, bring the needle up at the knot position. With the needle pointing away from you, twist the threads around it once. Put the needle down again where it emerged and pull through firmly, holding the thread taut with your left hand.

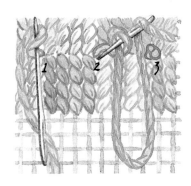

20 Star stitch variation

This complicated looking, and very decorative, pattern is simpler than it looks. Work the base star stitches first and then the big crosses over the top. Finish by anchoring down the centres of the cross stitches with straight stitches over 2 threads.

23 Plait stitch and tent stitch combination

Work a row of tent stitch, then plait, then tent stitch, and so on. The plait stitch rows are worked from left to right.

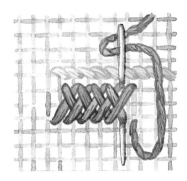

Stitch combinations

Use this as a true sampler and experiment with your own combinations and choice of threads. It is easier to stick to four or five colours to prevent the design becoming unbalanced, but there are no rules, so long as it is mapped out on graph paper before starting the finished result.

1 Rhodes stitch, see page 86
2 Straight stitch worked over 2 threads
3 Straight stitch and tent stitch, see page 94
4 Star stitch, overlaid with second colour
5 Byzantine stitch worked over 3 threads
6 Upright cross stitch, doubled, see page 94
7 Jacquard stitch worked over 1 and 3 threads
8 Christmas tree stitch and tent stitch, see page 94
9 Rice Stitch, see page 94
10 Fly stitch worked over 2 threads, divided by tent stitch, see page 95
11 Satin stitch squares worked over 4 threads. Each block is separated by backstitch

12 Diagonal straight stitch worked over 2 threads
13 Satin stitch squares worked over 3 threads, divided by backstitches worked over 3 threads
14 Gobelin stitch worked over 4 threads
15 Tent stitch worked over 4 threads, in alternate directions with French knots, see page 95
16 Cross stitch worked over 2 threads. Work the top stitches in alternate directions, see page 50
17 Straight stitch worked over 2 and 4 threads
18 Double oblong cross stitch worked over 2 threads with an extra straight stitch in between, see page 51
19 Cross stitch worked over 2 threads, see page 50
20 Star stitch variation, see page 95
21 Large cross stitch worked over 4 threads with double French knots
22 Straight stitch worked over 4 threads overlaid with backstitching worked over 3 threads
23 Plait stitch divided by tent stitch, see page 95
24 Reversed double cross stitch worked over 3 threads divided by tent stitch
25 Tent stitch worked in alternate directions overlaid with backstitch see page 22
26 Chequer stitch worked over 4 threads
27 Diagonal long stitch
28 Cross stitch combination worked over 4 threads
29 Fan stitch, see page 86
30 Half Milanese stitch
31 Hungarian stitch, see page 87
32 Milanese stitch, see page 87
33 Gobelin stitch
34 Diagonal tent stitch, see page 22
35 Fly stitch
36 Star stitch worked over 2 threads, see page 86

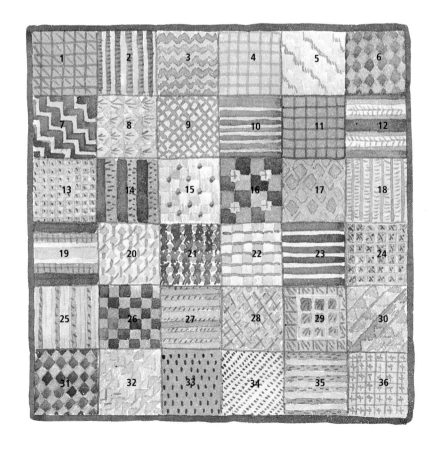

Charts & motifs

The following pages offer a range of additional charts and design motifs which will complement the projects in the earlier chapters, and provide inspiration for you to develop further needlepoint patterns of your own. They include charts and keys for two boat pictures: a steamer and a yacht and additional patterns for a hand and a heart cushion. Fruit, vegetables and flower motifs, a collection of counted border patterns and a selection of different backgrounds will all help you increase your needlepoint repertoire.

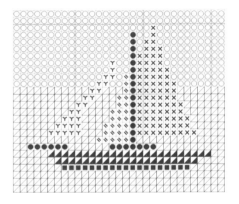

seaside pictures

See Boat pictures on page 24

Complete a trio of boat pictures by working these two designs, following the charts and keys for colours and threads. The motifs, near right, can be used, same size or enlarged, as single images or reduced to form a border for one of the boat pictures.

Steamer

Stranded cotton		Anchor	DMC	skeins
●	black	403	310	1
■	red	9046	817	1
⅄	brown	374	3828	1
◝	orange	316	971	1
○	sky grey	922	3768	1
╱	sea grey	851	924	1

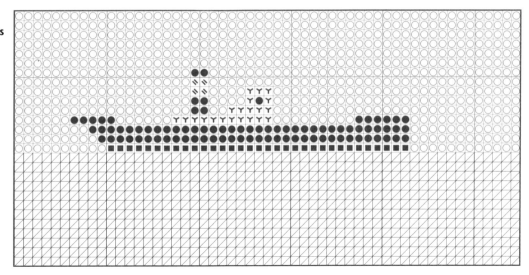

Yacht

Tapestry wool		Rowan	Anchor	skeins
■	maroon	H659	8512	1
◢	dirty pink	J412	8348	1
●	brown	X146	9392	1
✕	off-white	B84	9362	1
◝	cream	A2	8006	1
⅄	white	A110	8002	1
╱	sea blue	M415	8792	1
○	sky blue	M422	8834	1

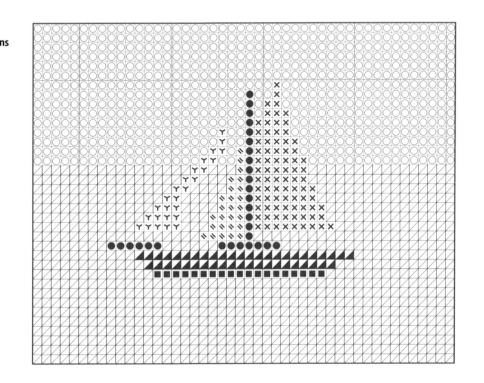

hand & heart

See House, heart & hand cushions on page 44

These additional patterns are for the hand and heart designs in this set of three cushions. Trace off the shapes and areas of stitch pattern and enlarge to your chosen size. Mark the outlines onto the canvas following the instructions on page 15. Use the same wool colours as for the house cushion , combining shades together to achieve a subtle faded effect.

fruit &
vegetables

This collection of fun motifs, similar in style to the teacosy on page 36, can be enlarged or reduced on a photocopier to the size of your choice. The motifs can then be used as a single design or arranged in groups to create free- style borders or overall patterns.

flower motifs

Flowers are ideal motifs for needlepoint. This selection of different blooms can be used in the size shown here, reduced for working on fine canvases for smaller projects such as pin cushions or enlarged to fit seat covers or pictures. Look at the colourings of the bobble-edged cushion, page 40, or the poppy slippers, page 56 , for inspiration when choosing wool colours for your flower pieces.

backgrounds

Large areas of background can be made more interesting both to stitch and to look at by adding some very simple patterning. It is a general rule that the yarn colours should not vary too greatly. However, with single 'dots' a high contrast, such as white dots on a dark background, can work really well. Choose the main needlepoint motif, then design a background that contrasts in colour and effect.

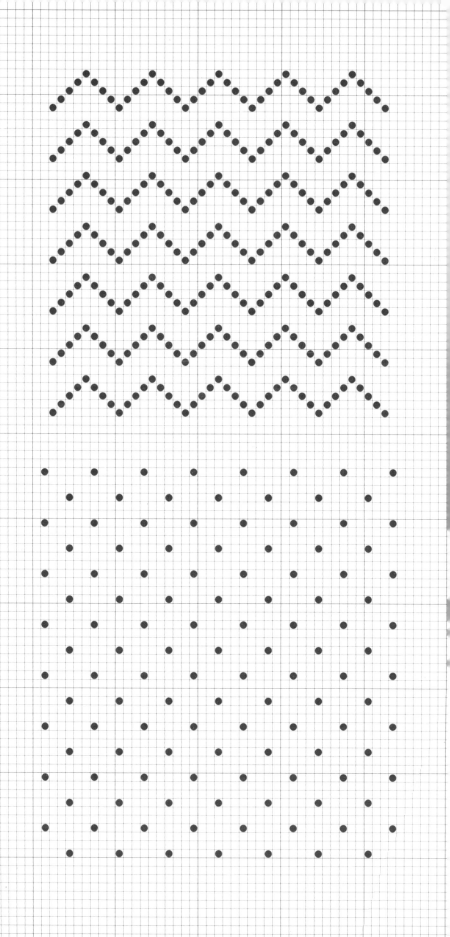

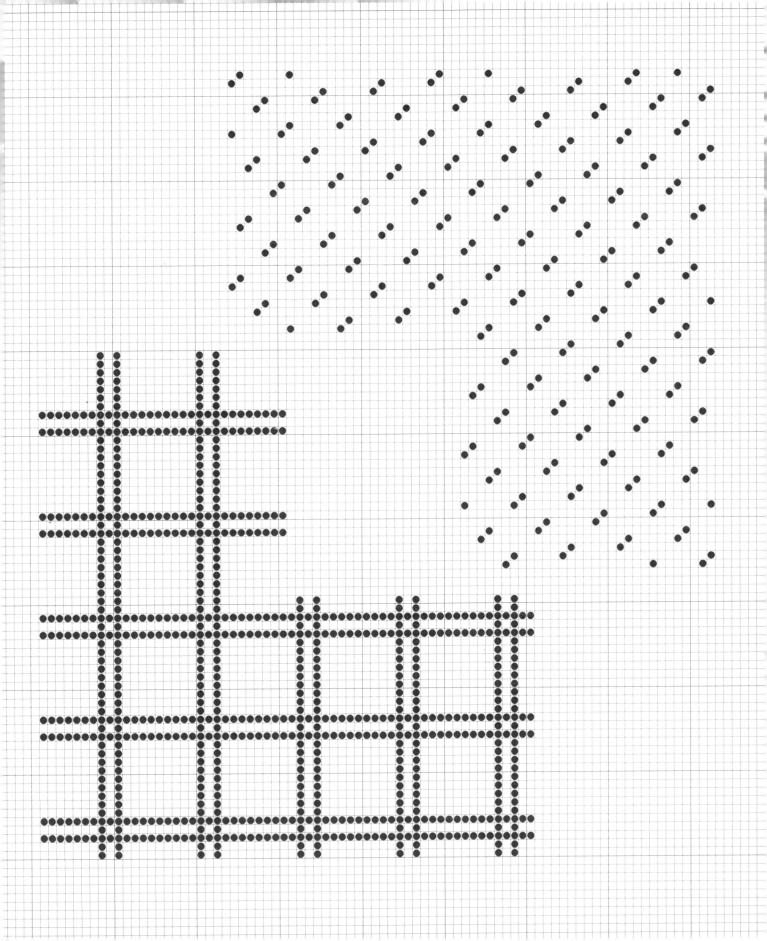

border patterns

This selection of repeating 'counted' border patterns can be translated in a variety of different ways. The patterns, near right, are based on single stitch arrangements, while the patterns on the far right, are long stitch designs. These patterns can also be used as all-over designs for cushion covers and chair seats, in a similar way to the kelim cushion on page 32 .

index

acknowledgments

The author would like to acknowledge Kathryn Whitefoot's invaluable assistance with the stitching of the sampler and the slippers. Thanks are also due to Sarah Ross Goobey for lending the antique needlepoint used for the chair seat, to Paterna Persian Yarn for stitching the art deco bag so beautifully, to Cara Ackerman at DMC, Julie Gill at Coats and Chris Hill who were extremely helpful in providing materials and technical advice.

The publisher would like to thank the designers and stitchers who contributed the following projects: Candace Bahouth for the Kelim cushion (page 32), DMC for stitching the Patchwork stool (page 66) from a design by Susan Duckworth, Jan Eaton for the Needlepoint bow (page 64), Lucinda Ganderton for the Album cover (page 30) and the House, heart & hand cushions (page 44), Jolly Red for the Circus cushion (page 26) and the Tea cosy (page 36), Gill Speirs (La Toison d'Or) for the Bobble-edged cushion (page 40) and the Cherub cushion (page 70), Victor Stuart Graham for the Boat pictures (page 24).
The Evening purse (page 88) and the Sampler (page 92) were designed and stitched by the author.

The publisher would also like to thank Christine Hanscomb for the use of her cottage as a location, Veronique Rolland for assisting the photographer and Antonia Gaunt (and her dog, Kivu) for the styling.